An Introduction to
Marxist Economic Theory

AN INTRODUCTION TO MARXIST ECONOMIC THEORY

by Ernest Mandel

PATHFINDER

New York   London   Montreal   Sydney

ISBN 978-0-87348-315-5
Library of Congress Catalog Card Number 73-82169
Manufactured in Canada

First Pathfinder edition, 1969
Second Pathfinder edition, 1973
Twenty-second printing, 2021

COVER PHOTO: Ed Weaver
This work was originally published in English by the Young Socialist
Alliance in 1967.

Pathfinder
www.pathfinderpress.com
E-mail: pathfinder@pathfinderpress.com

CONTENTS

INTRODUCTION
BY GEORGE NOVACK

The change in the social and political atmosphere of America in the last decade has intensified interest in Marxist ideas both among the general public and in university circles. For a long time, and especially during the reactionary cold-war era, it was an axiom of conventional wisdom that Marxism had become outdated. Some conceded that its teachings might retain value and validity for the colonial world but lacked any useful application to America today.

The main propositions of Marx, the argument went, essentially reflected the conditions of an immature stage of capitalist development belonging to the nineteenth century in the West. They no longer fitted the realities of such advanced capitalisms as the United States.

This opinion was voiced not only by conservative scholars and liberal commentators but by mentors of the New Left like C. Wright Mills who highly esteemed Marx's contributions to social thought and recommended them to students. Nevertheless, after reviewing the principal postulates of Marxism in his book *The Marxists,* the Columbia professor delivered the following verdict: "The political, psychological and economic expectations clearly derivable from his [Marx's] work seem increasingly unreal, his model as a whole increasingly inadequate. His theories bear the stamp of Victorian capitalism. . . ."

The contention that Marx's theories are irrelevant to our pressing national problems has become less and less fashionable and tenable as so many young people have begun to question the foundations and future of American capitalism. The teachings of Marxism seem cogent to them, not only because they have been adopted as a guide by the majority of progressive humanity and form an integral and indispensable element of contemporary thought and culture, but because they serve to explain the course taken by America's ruling class abroad and at home more profoundly and convincingly than any alternative system of ideas.

The author of this pamphlet has done much to promote this continuing shift of attitude toward Marxism. Ernest Mandel, editor-in-chief of the Belgian weekly *La Gauche*, is probably the most influential exponent of the political economy of scientific socialism in the Western world today.

He has taken a lead in the modernization of the Marxist heritage through his masterful two-volume work entitled *Marxist Economic Theory*. There he analyzes both neocapitalism and the postcapitalist societies in transition to socialism in a Marxist manner through the use of contemporary data and a critical examination of rival schools in this field.

This work has gone through several editions in France since it was first published there in 1962. It has been translated into many other languages, from English to Arabic.

Mandel has in addition contributed many articles on a broad range of subjects to periodicals throughout the world and has spoken at leading universities in the United States and Canada, although he has since been banned from the U.S., Germany, France, Switzerland, and Australia for his socialist views. This has brought widespread protest from scholars all over the world.

These are the resources which Ernest Mandel has drawn

on in this pamphlet, which was originally presented as a course during an educational weekend organized by the Paris Federation of the United Socialist Party in 1963. It has since been translated into several languages and extensively used in classes on the subject.

This is one of the most concise expositions of the elementary principles of Marxist political economy available. In the first section Mandel elucidates the basic categories of Marx's economic doctrines from the emergence of the social surplus-product to the labor theory of value. In the second he explains the laws of motion of the capitalist system and its inherent contradictions. In the final part he applies these concepts to the principal phenomena of the development of neocapitalism over the past forty years.

While Mandel, as a Trotskyist, adheres to classical Marxism, he does not rely on quotations or paraphrases from the standard Marxist works. His fresh and readable approach avoids the dullness often found in other treatments of these difficult topics.

The present edition includes new material in the form of an answer by Mandel to a criticism of his treatment of "socially necessary labor." Students who are looking for a clear and compact explanation of the dynamics of the capitalist system in our time will find it in these pages. For a more comprehensive and detailed exposition they should go on to read the two volumes of *Marxist Economic Theory*.

April 18, 1973

AUTHOR'S NOTE TO THE SECOND EDITION: ON SOCIALLY NECESSARY LABOR

Three Swedish authors claim that the double determination of socially necessary labor set forth in this work is the result of a confusion on the part of the author. According to them, of the two factors that determine socially necessary labor: (a) the average productivity of labor in a sector of production and (b) the effective social demand to be satisfied by the given commodity—only the first is valid. The second determines only the difference between the price and the value of commodities [Peter Dencik, Lars Herlitz, B-A Lundvall: *Marxismens politiske ekonomi—en introduktion,* Zenitserien 6, 1969, p. 25].

These critics are mistaken. In *Capital* (vol. 3, chap. 10) Marx explains how the two determinations of the "amount of socially necessary labor" should be combined. The necessity of the combination arises from the fact that value is a *social* category. The term "amount of socially necessary labor" poses a question: socially necessary to do what? Clearly to satisfy an effective demand. Without relating it to a need to be satisfied, the notion of "average productivity of a sector of industry," and even of "existing productive capacity" is meaningless in a system based on the generalized production of commodities where the entrepreneurs cannot realize surplus-value and accumulate capital unless they *sell* the commodities produced.

In this light, "average productivity" is neither a purely technical "fact," nor a mathematical average of the productive capacity of all the plants in a given branch of industry divided by the total number of producers employed. Rather, it fluctuates according to the relationship between productive capacity and sales. If two-thirds of the coal mines in a country are experiencing difficulty in selling their coal, work at only 50 percent of capacity, or even cease production, the "average productivity" of the coal industry will be very different from what it is when all the mines are working at full capacity, even if, in the meantime, no technical innovation is introduced into the industry.

Marx distinguishes three cases: (1) the case in which the value of a commodity is determined by plants working at the technological average productivity of the sector of industry (structural equilibrium of supply and demand); (2) the case in which the value of the commodity is determined by plants working at a level of productivity above the average for the sector of industry (supply structurally exceeds demand); (3) the case in which the value of the commodity is determined by plants working at a level of productivity below the average for the sector of industry (demand structurally exceeds supply) [*Capital*, (International Publishers, 1967), vol. 3, pp. 182–188]. In the first and third cases, the plants working under better conditions of productivity will realize surplus profit.

This is why Marx makes a distinction between "individual value" of commodities and "market value." In order not to complicate excessively the exposition contained in this pamphlet, which is only an introduction to Marxist economic theory, the author chose not to use the term "market value," while attempting, at the same time, to reproduce Marx's line of reasoning as clearly as possible.

The simple, abstract, total mass of living human labor expended at average intensity in the course of production determines the total mass of value newly created in society. This mass is predetermined in the process of production. It cannot be increased nor reduced by what happens on the market in the process of commodity circulation. But this rule holds only for society in its entirety. It is not valid for each sector of production, nor, *a fortiori*, for each plant. The market value may diverge from the "individual value," or the mass of abstract labor effectively contained in each commodity (redistribution of the mass of value and surplus-value within a sector). The prices of production may diverge from this market value (redistribution of value and surplus-value among several sectors).

Social needs play an important role in the mechanisms of redistribution of value and surplus-value. One of the essential functions of the "law of value" consists precisely of reestablishing over a period of time an equilibrium between the distribution of the material resources of society among different branches of production and the manner in which it divides its effective demand in order to satisfy its various needs (i.e., manner in which it measures and quantifies its needs under the antagonistic conditions of distribution characteristic of capitalist society), an equilibrium that generalized commodity production can never realize *a priori* nor directly.

|

The theory of
value and surplus-value

In the last analysis, every step forward in the history of civilization has been brought about by an increase in the productivity of labor. As long as a given group of men barely produced enough to keep itself alive, as long as there was no surplus over and above this necessary product, it was impossible for a division of labor to take place and for artisans, artists or scholars to make their appearance. Under these conditions, the technical prerequisites for such specialization could not possibly be attained.

SOCIAL SURPLUS PRODUCT

As long as the productivity of labor remains at a level where one man can only produce enough for his own subsistence, *social* division does not take place and any social differentiation within society is impossible. Under these conditions, all men are producers and they are all on the same economic level.

Every increase in the productivity of labor beyond this low point makes a small surplus possible, and once there is a surplus of products, once man's two hands can produce more than is needed for his own subsistence, then the conditions have been set for a struggle over how this surplus will be shared.

From this point on, the total output of a social group no longer consists solely of labor necessary for the subsistence of the producers. Some of this labor output may now be used to release a section of society from having to work for its own subsistence.

Whenever this situation arises, a section of society can become a ruling class, whose outstanding characteristic is its emancipation from the need of working for its own subsistence.

Thereafter, the labor of the producers can be divided into two parts. A part of this labor continues to be used for the subsistence of the producers themselves and we call this part *necessary labor;* the other part is used to maintain the ruling class and we give it the name *surplus labor.*

Let us illustrate this by the very clear example of plantation slavery, as it existed in certain regions and periods of the Roman Empire, or as we find it in the West Indies and the islands of Portuguese Africa starting with the seventeenth century, on the great plantations which were established there. In these tropical areas, even the slave's food was generally not provided by the master; the slave had to produce this himself by working a tiny plot of ground on Sundays and the products from this labor constituted his store of food. On six days of the week the slave worked on the plantation and received in return none of the products of his labor. This is the labor which creates a social surplus product, surrendered by the slave as soon as it is produced and belonging solely to the slavemaster.

The work week, which in this case is seven days, can be divided into two parts: the work of one day, Sunday, constitutes necessary labor, that labor which provides the products for the subsistence of the slave and his family; the work of the other six days is surplus labor and all of its products go to the master, are used for his sustenance and his enrichment as well.

The great domains of the early Middle Ages furnish us with another illustration. The land of these domains was divided into three parts: the communal lands consisting of forest, meadows, swamps, etc.; the land worked by the serf for his own and his family's subsistence; and finally, the land worked by the serf in order to maintain the feudal lord. The work week during this period was usually six days, not seven. It was divided into two equal parts: the serf worked three days on the land from which the yield belonged to him; the other three days he worked on the feudal lord's land, without remuneration, supplying free labor to the ruling class.

The products of each of these two very different types of labor can be defined in different terms. When the producer is performing necessary labor, he is producing a *necessary product.* When he is performing surplus labor, he is producing a *social surplus product.*

Thus, social surplus product is that part of social production which is produced by the laboring class but appropriated by the ruling class, regardless of the form the social surplus product may assume, whether this be one of natural products, or commodities to be sold, or money.

Surplus-value is simply the monetary form of the social surplus product. When the ruling class appropriates the part of society's production previously defined as "surplus product" exclusively in the monetary form, then we use the term "surplus-value" instead of "surplus product."

As we shall see later on, however, the above only constitutes a preliminary approach to the definition of surplus-value.

How does social surplus product come into existence? It arises as a consequence of a gratuitous appropriation, that is, an appropriation without compensation, by a ruling class of a part of the production of a producing class. When the slave worked six days a week on a plantation and the total product of his labor was taken by the master without any compensation to the slave, the origin of the social surplus product here is in the gratuitous labor, the uncompensated labor, supplied by the slave to the master. When the serf worked three days a week on the lord's land, the origin of this income, of this social surplus product, is also to be found in the uncompensated labor, the gratuitous labor, furnished by the serf.

We will see further on that the origin of capitalist surplus-value, that is to say, the revenue of the bourgeois class in capitalist society, is exactly the same: it is uncompensated labor, gratuitous labor, which the proletarian, the wage worker, gives the capitalist without receiving any value in exchange.

COMMODITIES, USE-VALUE AND EXCHANGE-VALUE

We have now developed several basic definitions which will be used throughout this exposition. A number of others must be added at this point.

Every product of human labor normally possesses utility; it must be able to satisfy a human need. We may therefore say that every product of human labor has a *use-value*. The term "use-value" will, however, be used in two different senses. We will speak of *the* use-value of a commodity;

we will also talk about use-values, as when we refer, for example, to a society in which only use-values are produced, that is to say, where products are created for direct consumption either by the producers themselves or by ruling classes which appropriate them.

Together with this use-value, a product of human labor can also have another value, an *exchange-value*. It may be produced for exchange on the market place, for the purpose of being sold, rather than for direct consumption by the producers or by wealthy classes. A mass of products which has been created for the purpose of being sold can no longer be considered as the production of simple use-values; it is now a production of *commodities.*

The commodity, therefore, is a product created to be exchanged on the market, as opposed to one which has been made for direct consumption. *Every commodity must have both a use-value and an exchange-value.*

It must have a use-value or else nobody would buy it, since a purchaser would be concerned with its ultimate consumption, with satisfying some want of his by this purchase. A commodity without a use-value to anyone would consequently be unsaleable, would constitute useless production, would have no exchange-value precisely because it had no use-value.

On the other hand, every product which has use-value does not necessarily have exchange-value. It has an exchange-value only to the extent that the society itself, in which the commodity is produced, is founded on exchange, is a society where exchange is common practice.

Are there societies where products do not have exchange-value? The basis for exchange-value, and *a fortiori* for trade and the market place, is constituted by a given degree of development of the division of labor. In order for products not to be directly consumed by their producers, it is essential that everybody should not be engaged in turning out the same thing. If a particular community has no division of labor, or only its most rudimentary form, then it is clear that no reason for exchange exists. Normally, a wheat farmer has nothing to exchange with another wheat farmer. But as soon as a division of labor exists, as soon as there is contact between social groups producing different use-values, then exchange can come about, at first on an occasional basis, subsequently on a more permanent one. In this way, little by little, products which are made to be exchanged, *commodities,* make their appearance alongside those products which are simply made for the direct consumption of their producers.

In capitalist society, commodity production, the production of exchange-values, has reached its greatest development. It is the first society in human history where the major part of production consists of commodities. It is not true, however, that all production under capitalism is commodity production. Two classes of products still remain simple use-value.

The first group consists of all things produced by the peasantry for its own consumption, everything directly consumed on the farms where it is produced. Such production for self-consumption by the farmer exists even in advanced capitalist countries like the United States, although it constitutes only a small part of total agricultural production. In general, the more backward the agriculture of a country, the greater is the fraction of agricultural production going for self-consumption. This factor makes it extremely difficult to calculate the exact national income of such countries.

The second group of products in capitalist society which are not commodities but remain simple use-value consists of all things produced in the home. Despite the fact that considerable human labor goes into this type of household production, it still remains a production of use-values and not of commodities. Every time a soup is made or a button sewn on a garment, it constitutes production, but it is not production for the market.

The appearance of commodity production and its subsequent regularization and generalization have radically transformed the way men labor and how they organize society.

THE MARXIST THEORY OF ALIENATION

You have no doubt already heard about the Marxist theory of alienation. The emergence, regularization and generalization of commodity production are directly related to the expanding character of this phenomenon of alienation.

We cannot dwell on this aspect of the question here but it is extremely important to call attention to it, since the history of trade covers far more than the capitalist era. It also includes *small-scale* commodity production, which we will discuss later. There is also a post-capitalist society based on commodities, a transitional society between capitalism and socialism, such as present-day Soviet society, for the latter still rests in very large measure on the foundations of exchange-value production. Once we have grasped certain fundamental characteristics of a society based on commodities, we can readily see why it is impossible to surmount certain phenomena of alienation in the transitional period between capitalism and socialism, as in Soviet society, for example.

Obviously this phenomenon of alienation does not exist—at least in the same form—in a society where commodity production is unknown and where the life of the individual and his social activity are united in the most elementary way. Man works, but generally not by himself; most often he is part of a collective group having a more or less organic structure. His labor is a direct transformation of material things. All of this means that labor activity, the act of production, the act of consumption, and the relations between the individual and his society are ruled by a condition of equilibrium which has relative stability and permanence.

We should not, of course, embellish the picture of primitive society, which was subject to pressures and periodic catastrophes because of its extreme poverty. Its equilibrium was constantly endangered by scarcity, hunger, natural disasters, etc. But in the periods between catastrophes, especially after agriculture had attained a certain degree of development and when climatic conditions were favorable, this kind of society endowed all human activities with a large degree of unity, harmony and stability.

Such disastrous consequences of the division of labor as the elimination of all aesthetic activity, artistic inspiration and creative activity from the act of production and the substitution of purely mechanical and repetitive tasks were nonexistent in primitive society. On the contrary, most of the arts, music, sculpture, painting, the dance, were originally linked to production, to labor. The desire to give an attractive and appealing form to products which were to be used either by the individual, his family, or larger kinship groups, found a normal, harmonious and organic expression within the framework of the day's work.

Labor was not looked upon as an obligation imposed from without, first of all because it was far less intense, far less exhausting than under capitalism today. It conformed more closely to the rhythms of the human organism as well as to the rhythms of nature. The number of working days per year rarely exceeded 150 to 200, whereas under capitalism the figure is dangerously close to 300 and sometimes even greater. Furthermore, there was a unity between the producer, his product and its consumption, since he generally produced for his own use or for those close to him, so that his work possessed a directly functional aspect. Modern alienation originates basically in the cleavage between the producer and his product, resulting both from the division of labor and commodity production. In other words, it is the consequence of working for the market, for unknown consumers, instead of for consumption by the producer himself.

The other side of the picture is that a society which only produces use-values, that is, goods which will be consumed directly by their producers, has always in the past been an impoverished society. Not only was it subject to the hazards of nature but it also had to set very narrow limits to man's wants, since these had to conform exactly to its degree of poverty and limited variety of products. Not all human wants are innate to man. There is a constant interaction between production and wants, between the development of the productive forces and the rise of new wants. Only in a society where labor productivity will be developed to its highest point, where an infinite variety of products will be available, will it be possible for man to experience a continuous expansion of his wants, a development of his own unlimited potential, an integrated development of his humanity.

THE LAW OF VALUE

One of the consequences of the appearance and progressive generalization of commodity production is that labor itself begins to take on regular and measurable characteristics; in other words, it ceases to be an activity tied to the rhythms of nature and according with man's own physiological rhythms.

Up to the nineteenth century and possibly even into the twentieth, the peasants in various regions of Western Europe did not work in a regulated way, that is to say, they did not work with the same intensity every month of the year. There were periods in the work year when they worked very hard and other periods, particularly during the winter, when all activity virtually came to a halt. It was in the most backward agricultural areas of most of the capitalist countries that capitalist society, in the course of its development, found a most attractive source of reserve manpower, for here was a labor force available for four to six months a year at much lower wages, in view of the fact that a part of its subsistence was provided by its agricultural activity.

When we look at the more highly developed and prosperous farms, those bordering the big cities, for example, and which are basically on the road to becoming industrialized, we see that work is much more regular and the amount of expended labor much greater, being distributed in a regular way throughout the year, with dead seasons progressively eliminated. This holds true not only for our times but even as early as the Middle Ages, at least from the twelfth century on. The closer we get to the cities, that is to say, to the marketplace, the more the peasant's labor becomes labor for the market, that is to say, commodity production, and the more regulated and more or less stable his labor becomes, just as if he were working inside an industrial enterprise.

Expressed another way, *the more generalized commodity production becomes, the greater the regulation of labor and the more society becomes organized on the basis of an accounting system founded on labor.*

When we examine the already fairly advanced division of labor within a commune at the beginning of commercial and craft development in the Middle Ages, or the collectives in such civilizations as the Byzantine, Arab, Hindu, Chinese and Japanese, certain common factors emerge. We are struck by the fact that a very advanced integration of agriculture and various craft techniques exists and that regularity of labor is true for the countryside as well as the city, so that an accounting system in terms of labor, in labor-hours, has become the force governing all the activity and even the very structure of the collectives. In the chapter on the law of value in my *Treatise on Marxist Economics,* I give a whole series of examples of this accounting system in work-hours. There are Indian villages where a certain caste holds a monopoly of the blacksmith craft but continues to work the land at the same time in order to feed itself. The rule which has been established is this: when a blacksmith is engaged to make a tool or weapon for a farm, the client supplies the raw materials and also works the blacksmith's land *during the whole period* that the latter is engaged in making the implement. Here is a very transparent way of stating that *exchange is governed by an equivalence in work-hours.*

In the Japanese villages of the Middle Ages, an accounting system in work-hours, in the literal sense of the term, existed inside the village community. The village accountant kept a kind of great book in which he entered the number of hours of work done by villagers on each others' fields, since agriculture was still mainly based on cooperative labor, with harvesting, farm construction and stock breeding being done in common. The number of work-hours furnished by the members of one household to the members of another was very carefully tallied. At the end of the year, the exchanges had to balance, that is, the members of household B were required to have given household A exactly the same number of work-hours which members of household A had given household B during the year. The Japanese even refined things to the point—almost a thousand years ago!—where they took into account that children provided a smaller quantity of labor than adults, so that an hour of child labor was "worth" only a half-hour of adult labor. A whole system of accounting was set up along these lines.

There is another example which gives us a direct insight into this accounting system based on labor-time: the conversion of feudal rent from one form to another. In feudal society, the agricultural surplus product could take three different forms: rent in the form of labor (the *corvee*), rent in kind, and money rent.

When a change is made from the corvee to rent in kind, obviously a process of conversion takes place. Instead of giving the lord three days of labor per week, the peasant now gives him a certain quantity of wheat, livestock, etc., on a seasonal basis. A second conversion takes place in the changeover from rent in kind to money rent.

These two conversions must be based on a fairly rigorous accounting in work-hours if one of the two parties does not care to suffer a loss in the process. For example, if at the time the first conversion was effected, the peasant gave the lord a quantity of wheat which required only 75 work-days of labor, whereas previously he had given the lord 150 work-days of labor in the same year, then this conversion of labor-rent into rent in kind would result in the sudden impoverishment of the lord and a rapid enrichment of the serfs.

The landlords—you can depend on them!—were careful

to see to it when the conversion was made that the different forms of rent were closely equivalent. Of course the conversion could eventually turn out to be a bad one for one of the participating classes, for example, against the landlords, if a sharp rise in agricultural prices occurred after rent was converted from rent in kind to money rent, but such a result would be historical in character and not directly attributable to the conversion *per se*.

The origin of this economy based on an accounting in labor-time is also clearly apparent in the division of labor within the village as it existed between agriculture and the crafts. For a long time the division remained quite rudimentary. A section of the peasantry continued to produce part of its own clothing for a protracted historical period, which in Western Europe extended almost a thousand years; that is, from the beginning of the medieval cities right up to the nineteenth century. The technique of making clothing was certainly no mystery to the cultivator of the soil.

As soon as a regular system of exchange between the farmer and textile craftsman was established, standard equivalents were likewise established—for example, an ell of cloth [a measure varying from 27 to 48 inches] would be exchanged for 10 pounds of butter, not for 100 pounds. Obviously the peasants knew, on the basis of their own experience, the approximate labor-time needed to produce a given quantity of cloth. Had there not been a more or less exact equivalence between the time needed to produce the cloth and the time needed to produce the butter for which it was exchanged, there would have been an immediate shift in the division of labor. If cloth production were more lucrative than butter production, the butter producers would switch to producing cloth. Since society here was only at the *threshold* of an extreme division of labor, that is to say, it was still at a point where the boundaries between different techniques were not clearly marked, the passage from one economic activity to another was still possible, particularly when striking material gains were possible by means of such a change.

In the cities of the Middle Ages as well, a very skillfully calculated equilibrium existed between the various crafts and was written into the charters which specified almost to the minute the amount of labor-time necessary for the production of different articles. It is inconceivable that under such conditions a shoemaker or blacksmith might get the same amount of money for a product which took half the labor-time which a weaver or other artisan might require in order to get the same amount of money for his products.

Here again we clearly see the mechanism of an accounting system in work-hours, a society functioning on the basis of an economy of labor-time, which is generally characteristic of the whole phase which we call *small-scale commodity production*. This is the phase intervening between a purely natural economy, in which only use-values are produced, and capitalist society, in which commodity production expands without limit.

DETERMINATION OF THE EXCHANGE-VALUE OF COMMODITIES

Once we have determined that the production and exchange of commodities becomes regular and generalized in a society based on an economy of labor-time, on an accounting system in work-hours, we can readily understand why the exchange of commodities, in its origins and inherent nature, rests on this fundamental basis of an accounting system in work-hours and consequently follows this general rule: *the exchange-value of a commodity is determined by the quantity of labor necessary to produce it.* The quantity of labor is measured by the length of time it takes to produce the commodity.

This general definition of the labor theory of value is the basis of both classical bourgeois political economy from the seventeenth century to the beginning of the nineteenth century, from William Petty to Ricardo; and Marxist economic theory, which took over the theory of labor value and perfected it. However, the general definition must be qualified in several respects.

In the first place, not all men are endowed with the same capacity for work, with the same strength or the same degree of skill at their trade. If the exchange-value of commodities depended only on the quantity of labor expended *individually,* that is, on the quantity of labor expended *by each individual* in the production of a commodity, we would arrive at this absurdity: the lazier or more incompetent the producer, and the larger the number of hours he would spend in making a pair of shoes, the greater would be the value of the shoes! This is obviously impossible since exchange-value is not a moral reward for mere willingness to work but *an objective bond set up between independent producers* in order to equalize the various crafts in a society based both on a division of labor and an economy of labor-time. In such a society wasted labor receives no compensation; on the contrary, it is automatically penalized. Whoever puts more time into producing a pair of shoes than the average necessary hours—an average determined by the average productivity of labor and recorded in the Guild Charters, for example!—such a person has wasted human labor, worked to no avail for a certain number of hours. He will receive nothing in exchange for these wasted hours.

Expressed another way, the exchange-value of a commodity is not determined by the quantity of labor expended by each individual producer engaged in the production of this commodity but by the quantity of labor *socially necessary* to produce it. The expression "socially necessary" means: the quantity of labor necessary under the average conditions of labor productivity existing in a given country at a given time.

The above qualification has very important applications when we examine the functioning of capitalist society more closely.

Another clarifying statement must be added here. Just what do we mean by a "quantity of labor"? Workers differ in their qualifications. Is there complete equality between one person's hour of work and everybody else's, regardless of such differences in skills? Once again the question is not a moral one but has to do with the internal logic of a society based on an equality between skills, an equality in the marketplace, and where any disruption of this equality would immediately destroy the social equilibrium.

What would happen, for example, if an hour's work by an unskilled laborer was worth as much as an hour's work by a skilled craftsman, who had spent four to six years as an apprentice in acquiring his skill? Obviously, no one would want to become skilled. The hours of work spent in learning a craft would be wasted hours since the craftsman would not be compensated for them after becoming qualified.

In an economy founded on an accounting system of work-hours, the young will desire to become skilled only if the time lost during their training period is subsequently paid for. Our definition of the exchange-value of a commodity must therefore be completed as follows: "An hour of labor by a skilled worker must be considered as complex labor, as compound labor, as a multiple of an hour of unskilled labor; the coefficient of multiplication obviously cannot be an arbitrary one but must be based on the cost of acquiring a given skill." It should be pointed out, in passing, that there was always a certain fuzziness in the prevailing explanation of compound labor in the Soviet Union under Stalin which has persisted to this very day. It is claimed that compensation for work should be based on the quantity *and quality* of the work, but the concept of quality is no longer understood in the Marxist sense of the term, that is to say, as a *quality measurable quantitatively* by means of a specific coefficient of multiplication. On the contrary, the idea of quality is used in the bourgeois ideological sense, according to which the quality of labor is supposed to be determined by its social usefulness, and this is used to justify the incomes of marshals, ballerinas and industrial managers, which are ten times higher than the incomes of unskilled laborers. Such a theory belongs in the domain of apologetics despite its widespread use to justify the enormous differences in income which existed under Stalin and continue to exist in the Soviet Union today, although to a lesser extent.

The exchange-value of a commodity, then, is determined by the quantity of labor socially necessary for its production, with skilled labor being taken as a multiple of simple labor and the coefficient of multiplication being a reasonably measurable quantity.

This is the kernel of the Marxist theory of value and the basis for all Marxist economic theory in general. Similarly, the theory of social surplus product and surplus labor, which we discussed at the beginning of this work, constitutes the basis for all Marxist sociology and is the bridge connecting Marx's sociological and historical analysis, his theory of classes and the development of society generally, to Marxist economic theory, and more precisely, to the Marxist analysis of all commodity-producing societies of a pre-capitalist, capitalist and post-capitalist character.

WHAT IS SOCIALLY NECESSARY LABOR?

A short while back I stated that the particular definition of the quantity of *socially* necessary labor for producing a commodity had a very special and extremely important application in the analysis of capitalist society. I think it will be more useful to deal with this point now although logically it might belong to a later section of this presentation.

The totality of all commodities produced in a country at a given time has been produced to satisfy the wants of the sum total of the members of this society. Any article which did not satisfy somebody's needs, which had no use-value for anyone, would be *a priori* unsaleable, would have no exchange-value, would not constitute a commodity but simply a product of caprice or the idle jest of some producer. From another angle, the sum total of buying power which exists in this given society at a given moment and which is not to be hoarded but spent in the market, must be used to buy the sum total of commodities produced, if there is to be economic equilibrium. This equilibrium therefore implies that the sum total of social production, of the available productive forces in this society, of its available work-hours, has been distributed among the various sectors of industry in the same proportions as consumers distribute their buying power in satisfying their various wants. When the distribution of productive forces no longer corresponds to this division in wants, the economic equilibrium is destroyed and both over-production and under-production appear side by side.

Let us give a rather commonplace example: toward the end of the nineteenth and beginning of the twentieth century, a city like Paris had a coach-building industry, which together with associated harness trades employed thousands or even tens of thousands of workers.

In the same period the automobile industry was emerging and although still quite small it already numbered some scores of manufacturers employing several thousands of workers.

Now what is the process taking place during this period? On the one hand, the number of carriages begins to decline and on the other, the number of automobiles begins to increase. The production of carriages and carriage equipment therefore shows a trend toward *exceeding social needs,* as these are reflected in the manner in which the inhabitants of Paris are dividing their buying power; on the other side of the picture, the production of automobiles is *below social needs,* for from the time the industry was launched until the advent of mass production, a climate of scarcity existed in this industry. The supply of automobiles on the market was never equal to the demand.

How do we express these phenomena in terms of the labor theory of value? We can say that in the carriage industry *more labor is expended than is socially necessary,* that a part of the labor expended by the sum total of companies in the carriage industry is socially wasted labor, which no longer finds an equivalent on the marketplace and is consequently producing unsaleable goods. In capitalist society, when goods are unsaleable it means that an investment of human labor has been made in a specific industrial branch *which turns out to be socially unnecessary labor,* that is to say, it is labor which finds no equivalent in buying power in the market-place. Labor which is not socially necessary is wasted labor; it is labor which produces no value. We can see from this that the concept of socially necessary labor embraces a whole series of phenomena.

For the products of the carriage industry, supply exceeds demand, prices fall and goods remain unsaleable. The reverse is true in the automobile industry where demand exceeds supply, causing prices to rise and under-production to exist. To be satisfied with these commonplaces about supply and demand, however, means stopping at the psychological and individual aspects of the problem. On the other hand, if we probe into the deeper social and collective side of the problem, we begin to understand what lies below the surface in a society organized on the basis of an economy of labor-time.

The meaning of supply exceeding demand is that capitalist production, which is anarchistic, unplanned and unorganized, has anarchistically invested or expended more labor hours in an industrial branch than are socially necessary, so that a whole segment of labor-hours turns out to be pure loss, so much wasted human labor which remains unrequited by society. Conversely, an industrial sector where demand continues to be greater than supply can be considered as an underdeveloped sector in terms of social needs; it is therefore a sector expending fewer hours of labor than are socially necessary and it receives a bonus from society in order to stimulate an increase in production and achieve an equilibrium with social needs.

This is one aspect of the problem of socially necessary labor in the capitalist system. The other aspect of the problem is more directly related to changes in the productivity of labor. It is the same thing but makes an abstraction of social needs, of the "use-value" aspect of production.

In capitalist society the productivity of labor is constantly changing. Generally speaking, there are always three types of enterprises (or industrial sectors): those which are technologically right at the social average; those which are backward, obsolete, on the downgrade, below the social average; and those which are technologically advanced and above average in productivity.

What do we mean when we say a sector or an enterprise is technologically backward and has a productivity of labor which is below the average? Such a branch or enterprise is analogous to our previously mentioned lazy shoemaker, that is, it is one which takes five hours to produce a specific quantity of goods in a period when the average social productivity demands that it be done in three hours. The two extra hours of expended labor are a total loss, a waste of social labor. A portion of the total amount of labor available to society having thus been wasted by an enterprise, it will receive nothing from society to compensate it. Concretely it means that the selling prices in this industry or enterprise, which is operating below average productivity, approach its production costs or even fall below them, that is to say, the enterprise is operating at a very low rate of profit or even at a loss.

On the other hand, an enterprise or industrial sector with an above average level of productivity (like the shoemaker who can produce two pairs of shoes in three hours when the social average is one pair per three hours) *economizes* in its expenditure of social labor and therefore makes a surplus profit, that is to say, the difference between its costs and selling prices will be greater than the average profit.

The pursuit of this surplus profit is, of course, the driving force behind the entire capitalist economy. Every capitalist enterprise is forced by competition to try to get greater profits, for this is the only way it can constantly improve its technology and labor productivity. Consequently all firms are forced to take this same direction, and this of course implies that what at one time was an above-average productivity winds up as the new average productivity, whereupon the surplus profit disappears. All the strategy of capitalist industry stems from this desire on the part of every enterprise to achieve a rate of productivity superior to the national average and thereby make a surplus profit, and this in turn provokes a movement which causes the surplus profit to disappear, by virtue of the trend for the *average* rate of labor productivity to rise continuously. This is the mechanism in the tendency for profit rates to become equalized.

THE ORIGIN AND NATURE OF SURPLUS-VALUE

And now, what is surplus-value? When we consider it from the viewpoint of the Marxist theory of value, the answer is readily found. Surplus-value is simply *the monetary form of the social surplus product,* that is to say, it is the monetary form of that part of the worker's production which he surrenders to the owner of the means of production without receiving anything in return.

How is this surrender accomplished in practice within capitalist society? It takes place through the process of exchange, like all important operations in capitalist society, which are always relations of exchange. The capitalist buys the labor-power of the worker, and in exchange for this wage, he appropriates the entire production of that worker, all the newly produced value which has been incorporated into the value of this production.

We can therefore say from here on that surplus-value is the difference between the value produced by the worker and the value of his own labor-power. What is the value of labor-power? In capitalist society, labor-power is a commodity, and like the value of any other commodity, its value is the quantity of labor socially necessary to produce and reproduce it, that is to say, the living costs of the worker in the wide meaning of the term. The concept of a minimum living wage or of an average wage is not a physiologically rigid one but incorporates wants which change with advances in the productivity of labor. These wants tend to increase parallel with the progress in technique and they are consequently not comparable with any degree of accuracy for different periods. The minimum living wage of 1830 cannot be compared quantitatively with that of 1960, as the theoreticians of the French Communist party have learned to their sorrow. There is no valid way of comparing the price of a motorcycle in 1960 with the price of a certain number of kilograms of meat in 1830 in order to come up with a conclusion that the first "is worth" less than the second.

Having made this reservation, we can now repeat that the living cost of labor-power constitutes its value and that surplus-value is the difference between this living cost and the value created by this labor-power.

The value produced by labor-power can be measured in a simple way by the length of time it is used. If a worker works ten hours, he produces a value of ten hours of work. If the worker's living costs, that is to say, the equivalent of his wage, is also ten hours of work, then no surplus-value would result. This is only a special case of the more general rule: when the sum total of labor product is equal to the product required to feed and maintain the producer, there is no social surplus product.

But in the capitalist system, the degree of labor productivity is such that the living costs of the worker are always less than the quantity of newly created value. This means that a worker who labors for ten hours does not need the equivalent of ten hours of labor in order to support himself in accordance with the average needs of the times. His equivalent wage is always only a fraction of his day's labor; everything beyond this fraction is surplus-value, free labor supplied by the worker and appropriated by the capitalist without an equivalent offset. If this difference did not exist, of course, then no employer would hire any worker, since such a purchase of labor-power would bring no profit to the buyer.

THE VALIDITY OF THE
LABOR THEORY OF VALUE

To conclude, we present three traditional proofs of the labor theory of value.

The first of these is the *analytical proof,* which proceeds by breaking down the price of a commodity into its constituent elements and demonstrating that if the process is extended far enough, only labor will be found.

The price of every commodity can be reduced to a certain number of components: the amortization of machinery and buildings, which we call the renewal of fixed capital; the price of raw materials and accessory products; wages; and finally, everything which is surplus-value, such as profit, rent, taxes, etc.

So far as the last two components are concerned, wages and surplus-value, it has already been shown that they are labor pure and simple. With regard to raw materials, most of their price is largely reducible to labor; for example, more than 60 per cent of the mining cost of coal consists of wages. If we start by breaking down the average manufacturing cost of commodities into 40% for wages, 20% surplus-value, 30% for raw materials and 10%

in fixed capital; and if we assume that 60% of the cost of raw materials can be reduced to labor, then we already have 78% of the total cost reduced to labor. The rest of the cost of raw materials breaks down into the cost of other raw materials—reducible in turn to 60% labor—plus the cost of amortizing machinery.

The price of machinery consists to a large degree of labor (for example, 40%) and raw materials (for example, 40% also). The share of labor in the average cost of all commodities thus passes successively to 83%, 87%, 89.5%, etc. It is obvious that the further this breakdown is carried, the more the entire cost tends to be reduced to labor, and to labor alone.

The second proof is the *logical proof,* and is the one presented in the beginning of Marx's *Capital.* It has perplexed quite a few readers, for it is certainly not the simplest pedagogical approach to the question.

Marx poses the question in the following way. The number of commodities is very great. They are interchangeable, which means that they must have a common quality, because everything which is interchangeable is comparable and everything which is comparable must have at least one quality in common. Things which have no quality in common are, by definition, not comparable with each other.

Let us inspect each of these commodities. What qualities do they possess? First of all, they have an infinite set of natural qualities: weight, length, density, color, size, molecular nature; in short, all their natural physical, chemical and other qualities. Is there any one of the physical qualities which can be the basis for comparing them as commodities, for serving as the common measure of their exchange-value? Could it be weight? Obviously not, since a pound of butter does not have the same value as a pound of gold. Is it volume or length? Examples will immediately show that it is none of these. In short, all those things which make up the natural quality of a commodity, everything which is a physical or chemical quality of this commodity, certainly determines its use-value, its relative usefulness, but not its exchange-value. Exchange-value must consequently be abstracted from everything that consists of a natural physical quality in the commodity.

A common quality must be found in all of these commodities which is not physical. Marx's conclusion is that the only common quality in these commodities which is not physical is their quality of being the products of human labor, of *abstract* human labor.

Human labor can be thought of in two different ways. It can be considered as specific concrete labor, such as the labor of the baker, butcher, shoemaker, weaver, blacksmith, etc. But so long as it is thought of as specific concrete work, it is being viewed in its aspect of labor which produces only use-values.

Under these conditions we are concerning ourselves only with the physical qualities of commodities and these are precisely the qualities which are not comparable. The only thing which commodities have in common from the viewpoint of exchanging them is that they are all produced by abstract human labor, that is to say, by producers who are related to each other on a basis of equivalence as a result of the fact that they are all producing goods for exchange. The common quality of commodities, consequently, resides in the fact that they are the products of abstract human labor and it is this which supplies the measure of their exchange-value, of their exchangeability. It is, consequently, the quality of socially necessary labor in the production of commodities which determines their exchange-value.

Let us immediately add that Marx's reasoning here is both abstract and difficult and is at least subject to questioning, a point which many opponents of Marxism have seized upon and sought to use, without any marked success, however.

Is the fact that all commodities are produced by abstract human labor really the *only* quality which they have in common, apart from their natural qualities? There are not a few writers who thought they had discovered others. In general, however, these have always been reducible either to physical qualities or to the fact that they are products of abstract labor.

A third and final proof of the correctness of the labor theory of value is the *proof by reduction to the absurd*. It is, moreover, the most elegant and most "modern" of the proofs.

Imagine for a moment a society in which living human labor has completely disappeared, that is to say, a society in which all production has been 100 per cent automated. Of course, so long as we remain in the current intermediate stage, in which some labor is already completely automated, that is to say, a stage in which plants employing no workers exist alongside others in which human labor is still utilized, there is no special theoretical problem, since it is merely a question of the transfer of surplus-value from one enterprise to another. It is an illustration of the law of equalization of the profit rate, which will be explored later on.

But let us imagine that this development has been pushed to its extreme and human labor has been completely eliminated from all forms of production and services. Can value continue to exist under these conditions? Can there be a society where nobody has an income but commodities continue to have a value and to be sold?

Obviously such a situation would be absurd. A huge mass of products would be produced without this production creating any income, since no human being would be involved in this production. But someone would want to "sell" these products for which there were no longer any buyers!

It is obvious that the distribution of products in such a society would no longer be effected in the form of a sale of commodities and as a matter of fact selling would become all the more absurd because of the abundance produced by general automation.

Expressed another way, a society in which human labor would be totally eliminated from production, in the most general sense of the term, with services included, would be a society in which exchange-value had also been eliminated. This proves the validity of the theory, for at the moment human labor disappears from production, value, too, disappears with it.

2

Capital and capitalism

CAPITAL IN PRECAPITALIST SOCIETY

Between primitive society founded on a natural economy in which production is limited to use-values destined for self-consumption by their producers, and capitalist society, there stretches a long period in human history, embracing essentially all human civilizations, which came to a halt before reaching the frontiers of capitalism. Marxism defines them as societies in which *small-scale commodity production* prevailed. A society of this kind is already familiar with the production of commodities, of goods designed for exchange on the market and not for direct consumption by the producers, but such commodity production has not yet become generalized, as is the case in capitalist society.

In a society founded on small-scale commodity production, two kinds of economic operations are carried out. The peasants and artisans who bring their products to market wish to sell goods whose use-value they themselves cannot use in order to obtain money, means of exchange, for the acquisition of other goods, whose use-value is either necessary to them or deemed more important than the use-value of the goods they own.

The peasant brings wheat to the marketplace which he sells for money; with this money he buys, let us say, cloth. The artisan brings his cloth to the market, which he sells for money; with this money he buys, let us say, wheat.

What we have here, then, is the operation: *selling in order to buy*. Commodity—Money—Commodity, $C-M-C$, which has this essential character: the value of the two extremes in this formula is, by definition, exactly the same.

But within small-scale commodity production there appears alongside the artisan and small peasant, another personage, who executes a different kind of economic operation. Instead of *selling in order to buy, he buys in order to sell*. This type of person goes to market without any commodities; he is an owner of money. Money cannot be sold; but it can be used to buy, and that is what he does: *buys in order to sell, in order to re-sell: $M-C-M'$*.

There is a fundamental difference between the two types of operation. The second operation makes no sense if upon its completion we are confronted by exactly the same value as we had at the beginning. No one buys a commodity in order to sell it for exactly the same price he paid for it. The operation "buy in order to sell" makes sense only if the sale brings a supplementary value, *a surplus-value*. That is why we state here, by way of definition: M' is greater than M and is made up of $M+m$; m being the surplus-value, the amount of increase in the value of M.

We now define *capital* as *a value which is increased by a surplus-value,* whether this occurs in the course of commodity circulation, as in the example just given, or in production, as is the case in the capitalist system. Capital, therefore, is every value which is augmented by a surplus-value; it therefore exists not only in capitalist society but in any society founded on small-scale commodity production as well. For this reason it is necessary to distinguish very clearly between the life of *capital* and that of the *capitalist mode of production,* of capitalist society. Capital is far older than the capitalist mode of production. The former probably goes back some 3,000 years, whereas the latter is barely 200 years old.

What form does capital take in precapitalist society? It is basically usury capital and merchant or commercial capital. The passage from precapitalist society into capitalist society is characterized by the penetration of capital into the sphere of production. The capitalist mode of production is the first mode of production, the first form of social organization, in which capital is not limited to the sole role of an intermediary and exploiter of noncapitalist forms of production, of small-scale commodity production. In the capitalist mode of production, capital takes over the means of production and penetrates directly into production itself.

ORIGINS OF THE CAPITALIST
MODE OF PRODUCTION

What are the origins of the capitalist mode of production? What are the origins of capitalist society as it has developed over the past 200 years?

They lie first of all in the separation of the producers from their means of production. Subsequently, it is the establishment of these means of production as a monopoly in the hands of a single social class, the bourgeoisie. And finally, it is the appearance of another social class which has been separated from its means of production and therefore has no other resources for its subsistence than the sale of its labor-power to the class which has monopolized the means of production.

Let us consider each of these origins of the capitalist mode of production, which are at the same time the fundamental characteristics of the capitalist system as well.

First characteristic: *separation of the producer from his means of production.* This is the fundamental condition for existence of the capitalist system but it is also the one which is generally the most poorly understood. Let us use an example which may seem paradoxical since it is taken from the early Middle Ages, which was characterized by serfdom.

We know that the mass of peasant-producers were serfs bound to the soil. But when we say that the serf was bound to the soil, we imply that the soil was also "bound" to the serf; that is, he belonged to a social class which always had a base for supplying its needs, enough land to work so that the individual serf could meet the needs of a household even though he worked with the most primitive implements. We are not viewing people condemned to death by starvation if they do not sell their labor-power. In such a society, there is *no economic compulsion* to hire out one's arms, to sell one's labor-power to a capitalist.

We can express this another way by stating that the capitalist system cannot develop in a society of this kind. This general truth also has a modern application in the way colonialists introduced capitalism into the African countries during the nineteenth and early twentieth centuries.

Let us look at the living conditions of the inhabitants in all the African countries. They were stock breeders and cultivators of the soil, on a more or less primitive basis, depending on the character of the region, but always under the condition of a relative abundance of land. Not only was there no scarcity of land in Africa, but in terms of the ratio of population to the amount of available land, it may be said that land reserves were virtually unlimited. It is true, of course, that the yield from these lands was mediocre because of the crude agricultural implements and the standard of living was very low, etc., but there was no material force pushing this population to work in the mines, on the farms or in the factories of the white colonialist. Without a transformation in the administration of land in Equatorial Africa, in Black Africa, there was no possibility for introducing the capitalist mode of production. For that, compulsion of a noneconomic character had to be used, a thoroughgoing and brutal separation of the black masses from their normal means of subsistence had to be carried out. A large part of the lands had to be transformed overnight into national domains, owned by the colonizing state, or into private property belonging to capitalist corporations. The black population had to be re-settled in domains, or in reserves, as they have been cynically called, in land areas which were inadequate for sustaining all their inhabitants. In addition, a head-tax, that is to say, a money tax on each inhabitant, was imposed as another lever, since primitive agriculture yielded no money income.

By these various extra-economic pressures, the colonialists created a need for the African to work for wages during perhaps two or three months a year, in order to earn the money to pay his tax and buy the small supplement of food necessary for his subsistence, since the land remaining at his disposal was no longer adequate for a livelihood.

In such countries as South Africa, the Rhodesias, and part of the former Belgian Congo, where the capitalist mode of production was introduced on a grand scale, these methods were applied on the same scale, and a large part of the black population was uprooted, expelled, and forced out of its traditional existence and mode of work.

Let us mention, in passing, the ideological hypocrisy which accompanied this movement, the complaints of the capitalist corporations that the blacks were lazy since they did not want to work even when they had a chance to make ten times as much in mines and factories as they did from their traditional labor on the land. These same complaints had been made about the Indian, Chinese and Arab workers some 50 to 70 years earlier. They were also made—a rather good proof of the basic equality of all the races which make up humanity—against the European workers, French, Belgian, English, German, in the seventeenth or eighteenth centuries. It is simply a function of this constant fact: normally, because of his physical and nervous constitution, no man cares to be confined for 8, 9, 10 or 12 hours a day in a factory, mill or mine; it really requires a most abnormal and unusual force or pressure to make a man engage in this kind of convict labor when he has not been accustomed to it.

A second origin and characteristic of the capitalist mode of production is this *concentration of the means of production in monopoly form and in the hands of a single social class, the bourgeoisie.* This concentration is virtually impossible unless a continual revolution is taking place in the means of production, in which the latter become increasingly complex and more costly, at least so far as the minimum means of production required for launching a big business (initial capital expenditures) are concerned.

In the guilds and trades of the Middle Ages, there was great stability in the means of production; the weaving-looms were transmitted from father to son, from generation to generation. The value of these looms was relatively small, that is to say, each journeyman could expect to get back the counter-value of these looms after a certain number of years of work. The possibility for establishing a monopoly arrived with the industrial revolution, which unleashed an uninterrupted development of increasingly complex mechanisms and concomitantly, a need for ever greater capital sums in order to start a new enterprise.

From this point on it may be said that access to the ownership of the means of production becomes impossible for the overwhelming majority of wage-earners and salaried personnel, and that such ownership became a monopoly in the hands of one social class, the class which possesses capital and capital reserves and can obtain additional capital by virtue of the single fact that it already has some of it. And by virtue of this same fact, the class without capital is condemned to remain perpetually in the same state of deprivation and consequently under the continuous compulsion to labor for somebody else.

The third origin and characteristic of capitalism: *the appearance of a social class which has no possessions save its own hands and no means of subsistence other than the sale of its labor-power,* but at the same time, is free to sell this labor-power and does so to the capitalist owners of the means of production. This is the appearance of the *modern proletariat.*

We have here three elements which combine with each other. The proletariat is the free worker; he constitutes both a step ahead and a step backwards, compared with the serf of the Middle Ages: a step ahead because the serf was not free (the serf was himself a step ahead compared with the slave) and could not move about freely; a step backwards because, in contrast with the serf, the proletarian has also been "liberated" from, that is to say, deprived of, all access to the means of production.

ORIGINS AND DEFINITION OF THE MODERN PROLETARIAT

Among the direct ancestors of the modern proletariat we must include the uprooted population of the Middle Ages which was no longer bound to the soil or incorporated in the trades, corporations and guilds of the free towns, and was consequently a wandering, rootless population, which had begun to sell its labor by the day or even by the hour. There were quite a few cities in the Middle Ages, notably Florence, Venice and Bruges, where a "labor market" appeared as early as the thirteenth, fourteenth, or fifteenth centuries. These cities had a place where the poor who did not belong to any craft, were not journeymen for an artisan and had no means of subsistence, assembled and waited to be hired by some merchant or businessman for an hour, half a day, a day, etc.

Another origin of the modern proletariat, closer to us in time, lies in what has been called the disbanding of the feudal retinues. It therefore corresponds with the long and slow decline of the feudal nobility, which set in during the thirteenth and fourteenth centuries and terminated with the bourgeois revolution in France at the end of the eighteenth century. In the remote Middle Ages, there were sometimes fifty, sixty to over a hundred households living directly from the feudal lord. The number of these individual attendants began to decline, especially during the sixteenth century, which was marked by a sharp rise in prices, and as a consequence, a great impoverishment of all those social classes with fixed money incomes. The feudal lords of Western Europe were also hard hit because most of them had converted rent in kind into money rent. One of the results of this impoverishment was a massive discharge of a substantial section of the feudal retinues. In this way thousands of former valets, servants, and clerks to the nobles became wanderers, beggars, etc.

A third origin of the modern proletariat comes from the expulsion of a part of the peasantry from its lands as a result of the transformation of these agricultural lands into grass-lands. The great English Utopian socialist Thomas More advanced this magnificent formula as far back as the sixteenth century: "Sheep have eaten men"; in other words, the transformation of fields into grass-lands for grazing sheep, as a result of the development of the wool industry, threw thousands upon thousands of English peasants off their lands and condemned them to starvation.

There is still a fourth origin of the modern proletariat, one which played a somewhat lesser role in Western Europe but an enormous one in Central and Eastern Europe, Asia, Latin America and North Africa: it is the destruction of the former artisans in the competitive struggle between the handicrafts and modern industry as the latter made its way into these under-developed countries from the outside.

In summary, the capitalist mode of production is a regime in which the means of production have become a monopoly in the hands of a social class and in which the producers, separated from these means of production, are free but are deprived of all means of subsistence and consequently must sell their labor-power to the owners of these means of production in order to subsist.

What is characteristic of the proletarian therefore is not the level of his wage, whether this be high or low, but primarily the fact that he has been cut off from his means of production, or that his income is insufficient for him to work for his own account.

In order to learn whether the proletarian condition is on the road to disappearing or whether, on the contrary, it is on the road of expansion, it is not so much the average wage of the worker or the average salary of the clerk which we must examine, but this wage or salary as compared with his average consumption; in other words, we must look into his possibilities for savings and compare them with the expenses of setting up an independent enterprise. If we determine that each worker, each clerk, can, after ten years of work, put aside a pile of savings which would allow him to purchase a store or small workshop, then we might say that the proletarian condition is regressive and that we live in a society in which property in the means of production is spreading and becoming generalized.

If we find, however, that the overwhelming majority of workers, manual, white-collar and governmental, remain the same poor fellows after a life of labor that they were before, in other words with no savings or not enough capital to buy means of production, we may conclude that the proletarian condition has become generalized rather than contracted, and that it is far more prevalent today than it was 50 years ago. When we examine statistics on the social structure of the United States, for example, we can see that over the past 60 years, there has been an uninterrupted decrease every five years in the percentage of the active American population working for its own account and classified as businessmen or working in a family business, whereas the percentage of this same population which is compelled to sell its labor-power has steadily increased.

Moreover, if we examine the statistics on the distribution of private wealth, we find that the overwhelming majority of workers, we may say 95 per cent, and the very great majority of white-collar workers (80 or 85 per cent) are not even able to amass petty sums, small capitals; in other words, these groups expend their entire incomes. Fortunes are in reality limited to a very small fraction of the population. In most capitalist countries, 1%, 2%, 2.5%, 3.5% or 5% of the population possess 40%, 50%, 60% of the private wealth of the country, the balance being in the hands of 20% or 25% of this same population. The first category of possessors is the big bourgeoisie; the second category is the middle and petty-bourgeoisie. And all those who are outside these categories own nothing but consumer goods (sometimes including their housing).

When honestly compiled, statistics on estate duties and inheritance taxes are very revealing on this subject.

A specific study made by the Brookings Institute (a source above any suspicion of Marxism) for the New York Stock Exchange reveals that only one or two per cent of workers own stocks and further that this "ownership" averages about $1,000 worth.

Virtually all capital is therefore in the hands of the bourgeoisie and this reveals the self-reproductive character of the capitalist system: those who possess capital keep on accumulating more and more; those who do not possess it rarely can acquire it. In this way the division in society is perpetuated in a possessing class and a class compelled to sell its labor-power. The price for this labor-power, the wage, is virtually consumed *in toto*, whereas the possessing class has a capital constantly increasing from surplus-value. Society's enrichment in capital therefore takes place, so to speak, for the exclusive profit of a single social class, namely, the capitalist class.

THE FUNDAMENTAL MECHANISM
OF CAPITALIST ECONOMY

And now what is the functioning basis of this capitalist society?

If you were to go to the Printed Cottons Exchange on a certain day, you would not know whether there was exactly enough, or too little, or too much printed cottons, measured against the existing needs in France at that moment. You would only find that out after a certain time: that is to say, if there were overproduction and a part of production unsaleable, you would see prices fall. If there were, on the contrary, a scarcity, you would see prices rise. The movement of prices is the thermometer telling us whether there is a scarcity or plethora. And since it is only after the event that we find out whether the quantity of labor expended in an industrial branch has been expended in a socially necessary way or whether part of it has been wasted, it is only after the event that we are able to determine the exact value of a commodity. This value, therefore, is, if you choose to call it so, an abstraction; but it is a real constant around which prices fluctuate.

What causes the movement in these prices and consequently, in longer terms, the movement in these values, in this labor productivity, in this production and in this overall economic life?

What makes Sammy run? What causes capitalist society to move? *Competition.* Without competition there is no capitalist society. A society where competition is radically or completely eliminated would no longer be capitalist to the extent that there would no longer be a major economic motive for accumulating capital and consequently for carrying out nine-tenths of the economic operations which capitalists execute.

And what is the basis of competition? Two ideas are basic to it but these do not necessarily overlap. First is the idea of the *unlimited market,* the market without restrictions, without exact boundaries. Then there is the idea of a *multiplicity of decision centers,* above all in matters of investment and production.

If all production in a given industrial sector were concentrated in the hands of a single capitalist firm, competition would still not be eliminated, because an unlimited market would still exist and there would still be a competitive struggle between this industrial sector and other sectors to capture as much of this market as possible. Furthermore, there would always be a possibility that a foreign competitor might enter the scene and provide new competition right in the very same sector.

The reverse is also true. If we can conceive a totally and completely limited market, but one in which a great number of enterprises are fighting to capture a part of this limited market, then competition must obviously survive.

Therefore only if these two phenomena were to be suppressed simultaneously, that is to say, if there were only one producer for all commodities and the market became absolutely stable, frozen and without any capacity for expansion, could competition disappear completely.

The appearance of the unlimited market displays all of its significance when compared with the period of small-scale commodity production. A guild in the Middle Ages generally worked for a market limited to the city and its immediate suburbs, and in accordance with fixed and specific labor techniques.

The historical passage of the limited market to the unlimited market is illustrated by the example of the "new clothiers" of the countryside which replaced the old city clothiers in the fifteenth century. There were now cloth manufacturers without guild regulations, without production limits, therefore without any market restrictions, who tried to infiltrate everywhere, seek clients everywhere, and not only went beyond the immediate area of their production centers, but even tried to organize an export trade to very distant countries. On the other hand, the great commercial revolution of the sixteenth century stimulated a relative reduction in the prices of a whole set of products which had been considered great luxuries in the Middle Ages and were only within the purchasing range of a small part of the population. These products suddenly became far less expensive, and even came within the reach of a significant part of the population. The most striking example of this trend is sugar, which has become a commonplace product today and is undoubtedly to be found in every working-class household in France or in Europe; in the fifteenth century, however, it was still a highly luxurious article.

The apologists for capitalism have always pointed to the reduction in prices and widened market for a whole set of products as the benefits brought about by this system. This argument is true. It is one of the aspects of what Marx called "the civilizing mission of Capital." To be sure we are concerned here with a dialectical but real phenomenon where the value of labor-power has a tendency to fall by virtue of the fact that capitalist industry produces the commodity equivalent of wages with ever increasing rapidity while it simultaneously has a tendency to rise by virtue of the fact that this value of labor-power progressively takes in the value of a whole series of commodities which have become mass consumer goods, whereas formerly they were reserved for a very small part of the population.

Basically, *the entire history of trade between the sixteenth and twentieth century is the history of a progressive transformation from trade in luxury goods into trade in mass consumer goods;* into trade in goods destined for an ever increasing portion of the population. It is only with the development of the railroads, of the means for fast navigation, of telegraphy, etc., that it became possible for the whole world to be marshaled into a real potential market for each great capitalist producer.

The idea of an unlimited market does not, therefore, merely imply geographic expansion, but economic expansion, available purchasing power, also. To take a recent example: the extraordinary rise in the production of durable consumer goods in world capitalist production during the past fifteen years was not at all due to any geographic expansion of the capitalist market; on the contrary, it was accompanied by a geographic reduction in the capitalist market, since a whole series of countries were lost to it during this period. There are few, if any, automobiles of French, Italian, German, British, Japanese or American manufacture exported to the Soviet Union, China, North Vietnam, Cuba, North Korea, or the countries of East Europe. Nevertheless, this expansion did take place, thanks to the fact that a much greater fraction of the available purchasing power, which had increased absolutely as well, was used for buying these durable consumer goods.

It is no accident that this expansion has been accompanied by a more or less permanent agricultural crisis in industrially advanced countries, where the consumption of a whole group of agricultural products has not only ceased to increase on a relative basis but is even beginning to show an absolute decline: for example, the consumption of bread, potatoes, and of commonplace fruits like apples, pears, etc.

Production for an unlimited market, under competitive conditions, results in increased production, for an increase in production permits a reduction in costs and affords the means for beating a competitor by underselling him.

If we look at the long-term change in the value of all commodities which are produced on a large scale in the capitalist world, there can be no doubt that their value has declined considerably. A dress, knife, pair of shoes, or schoolboy's notebook today has a value in hours and minutes of labor which is far lower than it was fifty or a hundred years ago.

Obviously real production values must be compared and not sale prices, which include either enormous distribution and sales expenses or swollen monopolistic super-profits. Using gasoline as an example, especially the gasoline distributed in Europe and originating in the Middle East, we find that its production costs are very low, barely 10 per cent of the sale price.

In any event, there can be no doubt about the fact that this drop in value has actually taken place. Growth in labor productivity means a reduction in the value of goods, since the latter are manufactured with an ever reduced quantity of labor-time. Therein lies the practical tool which capitalism possesses for enlarging its markets and defeating its competitors.

What practical method does the capitalist have for sharply cutting his production costs and simultaneously sharply increasing his production? It is the *development of mechanization,* the development of means of production, mechanical instruments of labor of ever increasing complexity, originally powered by steam power, then by gasoline or diesel oil, and finally by electricity.

THE GROWTH IN THE ORGANIC COMPOSITION OF CAPITAL

All capitalist production can be represented in value by the formula: $C+V+S$. The value of every commodity consists of two parts: one part represents *crystallized or conserved value* and the other *newly created value.* Labor-power has a dual function, a dual use-value: that of preserving all existing values in the instruments of labor, machines, buildings, while incorporating a fraction of this value into current production; and that of creating a new value, which contains surplus-value, profit, as one of its components. Another part of this new value goes to the worker, and represents the counter-value of his wage. The surplus-value portion is appropriated by the capitalist without any counter-value.

We call the equivalent of wages variable capital and designate it by V. Why is it capital? Because, in effect, the capitalist advances this value; it constitutes, therefore, a part of his capital, which is expended before the value of the commodities produced by the workers in question can be realized.

We call that part of capital which is transformed into machines, buildings, raw materials, etc., whose value is not increased by production but merely preserved by it, constant capital and designate it by C. The part of capital called variable capital, V, the part used by the capitalist to buy labor-power, is so termed because it is the only part of capital which lets the capitalist increase his capital by means of a surplus-value.

Since this is the case, what is the economic logic of competition, of the drive to increase productivity, to increase mechanical means, machine labor? The logic of this drive, that is to say, the fundamental tendency of the capitalist system, is to increase the weight of C, the weight of constant capital, with respect to variable capital. In the fraction $\frac{C}{V}$, C tends to increase, that is to say, the part of total capital made up by machines and raw materials, but not in wages, tends to increase with the advances in mechanization and wherever competition compels capitalism to step up labor productivity.

We call this fraction $\frac{c}{v}$ the organic composition of capital: it is therefore the ratio between constant capital and variable capital, and we say that in the capitalist system this organic composition has a rising tendency.

How can the capitalist acquire new machines? What is the meaning of the statement that constant capital keeps on increasing?

The fundamental operation of capitalist economy is the production of surplus-value. But so long as the surplus-value has merely been produced, it remains locked in the commodities and the capitalist cannot use it; unsold shoes cannot be transformed into new machines, into greater productivity. In order to be able to buy new machines, the industrialist possessing shoes must sell these shoes, and a part of the proceeds of this sale can then serve to purchase new machines, as a supplementary constant capital.

Expressed another way: *realizing surplus-value is the necessary condition for the accumulation of capital,* and capital accumulation is simply the capitalization of surplus-value.

Realizing surplus-value means the sale of goods but also the sale of such goods under conditions where the surplus-value they contain can actually be realized in the market. All businesses operating at average productivity in society—whose total production therefore corresponds with socially necessary labor—are supposed to realize the total value and surplus-value produced in their plants, neither more nor less, when their goods are sold. We saw previously that those enterprises which are above the average in their productivity will capture a part of the surplus-value produced in other enterprises, whereas those operating at a lower than average productivity will not realize a part of the surplus-value produced in their plants but must surrender it to other plants which are technologically ahead of them. Consequently, the realization of surplus-value means the sale of goods under conditions in which all of the surplus-value produced by the workers in a plant manufacturing commodities is actually paid for by their purchasers.

As soon as the stock of goods produced in a given period is sold, the capitalist is reimbursed with a sum of money which constitutes the counter-value of the constant capital expended in achieving this production, that is to say, the raw materials used together with the fraction of the value of machines and goods amortized by this production. He has also been reimbursed with the counter-value of wages which he advanced in order to effect this production. In addition, he is in possession of the surplus-value produced by his workers.

What happens to this surplus-value? A part of it is *unproductively consumed* by the capitalist, for the poor fellow has to live, has to keep his family alive together with his entourage; and everything he spends for these purposes is completely withdrawn from the process of production.

A second part of the surplus-value is accumulated and is utilized by being transformed into capital. Accumulated surplus-value is, consequently, that entire part of surplus-value which is not unproductively consumed in meeting the private needs of the ruling class, and which is transformed into capital, either into supplementary constant capital, that is to say, into a supplementary quantity (more exactly: a value) of raw materials, machines, buildings; or into supplementary variable capital, that is to say, means for hiring more workers.

We now understand why the accumulation of capital is the capitalization of surplus-value, that is to say, the transformation of a large part of surplus-value into supplementary capital. And we also understand how the process of growth in the organic composition of capital represents an uninterrupted succession of capitalization processes, that is to say, of the production of surplus-value by workers and its transformation by the capitalists into supplementary buildings, machines, raw materials and workers.

It is consequently inaccurate to say that it is the capitalist who creates employment, since it is the worker who produced the surplus-value, which was capitalized by the capitalist, and used, among other things, for hiring more workers. In reality, the entire mass of fixed wealth we see in the world, the whole mass of plants, machines, roads, railroads, ports, hangars, etc., etc., all of this enormous mass of wealth is nothing but the materialization of a mass of surplus-value created by the workers, of nonreimbursed labor which was transformed into private property, into capital for the capitalists. It is, in other words, a colossal proof of the continuous exploitation undergone by the working class since the origin of capitalist society.

Do all capitalists progressively add machines, increase their constant capital and the organic composition of their capital? No, the increase in the organic composition of capital takes place antagonistically, by way of a competitive struggle governed by that law which the great Flemish painter, Peter Breughel, portrayed in an engraving: *the big fish eat the little.*

The competitive struggle is therefore accompanied by a continuous concentration of capital, by the displacement of a large number of businessmen by a smaller number, and by the transformation of a certain number of independent business people into technicians, managers, foremen, and even simple subordinate office personnel and workers.

COMPETITION LEADS TO
CONCENTRATION AND MONOPOLY

The concentration of capital is another permanent law of capitalist society and is accompanied by the proletarianization of a part of the bourgeois class, the expropriation of a certain number of bourgeois by a smaller number of bourgeois. That is why the *Communist Manifesto* of Marx and Engels emphasizes the fact that capitalism, which claims to defend private property, is in reality a destroyer of this private property, and carries out a constant, permanent expropriation of a great number of proprietors by a relatively small number of proprietors. There are several industrial branches in which this concentration is particularly striking: coal mining had hundreds of companies during the nineteenth century in a country like France (there were almost two hundred in Belgium); the automobile industry had a hundred or more firms at the beginning of the century in countries like the United States and England, whereas today their number has been reduced to four, five or six such companies at most.

Of course, there are industries where this concentration has not been carried so far, such as the textile industry, the food industry, etc. In general, the greater the organic composition of capital in an industrial branch, the greater is the concentration of capital, and conversely, the smaller the organic composition of capital, the smaller is the concentration of capital. Why? Because the smaller the organic composition of capital, the less capital is required at the beginning in order to enter this branch and establish a new venture. It is far easier to put together the million or two million dollars necessary for building a new textile plant than to assemble the hundreds of millions needed to set up even relatively small steel works.

Capitalism was born of free competition and is inconceivable without competition. But free competition produces concentration, and concentration produces the opposite of free competition, namely, monopoly. Where there are few producers, they can readily reach agreements, at the expense of the consumers, in dividing up markets and preventing any lowering of prices.

So in the span of a century, the whole capitalist dynamic appears to have changed its nature. First we have a movement proceeding in the direction of a constant fall in prices because of a constant rise in production and a constant multiplication of the number of enterprises. At a certain point, the sharpening of competition brings with it a concentration of enterprises and a reduction in the number of enterprises. The remaining companies are now able to reach agreement on preventing further price reductions and such agreement can only be honored, of course, by limiting production. The era of monopoly capitalism thus displaces the era of free competitive capitalism at the beginning of the last quarter of the nineteenth century.

Naturally, when we speak of monopoly capitalism, we must not in the least presume a capitalism which has completely eliminated competition. There is no such thing. We simply mean a capitalism whose basic behavior has changed, that is to say, it no longer strives for a constant lowering of prices by means of a constant increase in production; it uses the technique of dividing up the market, of setting up market quotas. But this process winds up in a paradox. Why do capitalists who began as competitors now turn to concerted action in order to limit this competition and to limit production as well? The answer is that it is a method of increasing their profits. They only do so if it brings them more profits. Limiting production permits increasing prices, bringing greater profits and consequently increased capital accumulation.

This new capital can no longer be invested in the same branch, since this would mean an increase in productive capacity, resulting in increased production, and leading to a lowering of prices. Capitalism has been caught up in this contradiction commencing with the last quarter of the nineteenth century. It then suddenly acquired a quality which only Marx had foreseen and which was not grasped by economists like Ricardo or Adam Smith; suddenly, the capitalist mode of production took on a missionary role. It began to spread throughout the world by means of *capital exports,* which enabled capitalist enterprises to be set up in countries or sectors where monopolies had not yet entrenched themselves.

The consequence of monopoly in certain branches and of the spread of monopoly capitalism in certain countries is that the capitalist mode of production has been reproduced in branches still free from monopoly control and in countries which had not yet become capitalist. This is how colonialism in all its varieties managed, toward the beginning of the twentieth century to spread like a powder train in the course of a few decades, starting from the small part of the world to which the capitalist mode of production was limited, and eventually embracing the whole world. Every country on the map was thus transformed into a sphere of influence and field of investment for capital.

TENDENCY OF THE AVERAGE RATE OF PROFIT TO DECLINE

We saw previously that the surplus-value produced by the workers in each factory remained "locked" in the products, and that the question whether or not this surplus-value would be realized by the capitalist factory owner was decided by market conditions, that is to say, by the possibility for the factory to sell its products at a price which would allow all of this surplus-value to be realized. By applying the law of value developed earlier, we can set up the following rule: all enterprises which are producing at the average level of productivity will, roughly speaking, realize the surplus-value produced by their workers, that is to say, they will sell their products at a price equal to the value of these products.

But this will not be the case for two categories of enterprises: those operating below and those operating above the average level of productivity.

What is the category of enterprises operating below the average level of productivity? This is nothing but a generalization of the lazy shoemaker we mentioned previously. It is, for example, a steel mill which produces 500,000 tons of steel in 2.2 or 2.5 or 3 million man-hours, when the national average for this production is 2 million man-hours. It is therefore wasting social labor-time. The surplus-value produced by the workers in this factory will not be realized in its entirety by the owners of this plant; it will work at a profit below the average rate of profit for all enterprises in the country.

But the total mass of surplus-value produced in society is a fixed mass, dependent in the last analysis on the total number of labor hours supplied by all workers engaged in production. This means that if there are a certain number of enterprises which do not realize all the surplus-value produced by their workers because the enterprises are operating below the average level of productivity and have therefore wasted social labor-time, then there is an unexpended balance of surplus-value available which is captured by the plants operating above the average level of productivity. Having economized on social labor-time, the latter are rewarded by society.

This theoretical explanation is a general demonstration of the mechanism determining the movement of prices in capitalist society. How does this mechanism operate in practice?

Let us say the average selling price of a locomotive is a million dollars. What then will be the difference between a plant operating below the average productivity of labor and one operating above it? The first will spend, let us say, $900,000 to produce a locomotive, and its profit will be $100,000. On the other hand, the plant producing above the average level of labor productivity, will spend, let us say, $750,000 and will make $250,000 profit, that is 33 per cent on its current production, whereas the average rate of profit is 18 per cent and enterprises working at this average social labor productivity produced locomotives at a cost of $850,000, realizing $150,000 in profit, that is to say, 18 per cent.[1]

In other words, capitalist competition favors those enterprises which are technologically ahead; these enterprises realize *superprofits* as compared with the average profit. Average profit is basically an abstract idea, exactly like value. It is an average around which the real profit rates of different branches and enterprises fluctuate. Capital flows toward the branches where there are superprofits and flows away from those branches in which profits are below the average. By virtue of this ebb and flow of capital from one branch to another, the rates of profit tend to approximate this average, without ever completely reaching

---

1. In reality, the capitalists do not figure their profit rate on the basis of current production, but on their invested capital; in order to avoid complicated calculations, we can imagine that the entire capital is absorbed in the production of one locomotive.

it in an absolute and mechanical way.

This is the way then that equalization of the rates of profit is effected. There is a very simple way to determine this abstract average rate of profit: we take the total mass of surplus-value produced by all workers in a given year and in a given country, and draw its ratio to the total mass of capital investment in that country.

What is the formula for the rate of profit? It is the ratio between surplus-value and total capital. It is therefore $\frac{S}{C+V}$. Still another formula must be considered as well: $\frac{S}{V}$; this is the *rate of surplus-value,* or better still, the *rate of exploitation of the working class.* It specifies the way in which the newly produced value is divided between workers and capitalists. If, for instance, $\frac{S}{V}$ equals 100 per cent this means that the newly produced value is divided into two equal parts, one part going to the workers in the form of wages, the other going to the bourgeois class in the form of profits, interest, dividends, etc.

When the exploitation rate of the working class is 100 per cent, the 8-hour working day then consists of two equal parts: 4 hours of labor in which the workers produce the counter-value of their wages, and 4 hours in which they supply gratuitous labor, labor which is not paid for by the capitalists and its product appropriated by the latter.

At first sight, it seems that if the organic composition of capital $\frac{C}{V}$ increases, the profit rate $\frac{S}{C+V}$ will decline, since C becomes increasingly greater relative to V, and S is a product of V and not of C. But there is a factor that can neutralize the effect of an increase in the organic composition of capital: it is precisely an increase in the surplus-value rate.

If S over V, the surplus-value rate increases, this means that in the fraction $\frac{S}{C+V}$, both the numerator and denominator increase, and in this case the value of the fraction can remain the same, under conditions where the two increases occur in a certain proportion.

In other words, an increase in the surplus-value rate can neutralize the effects of an increase in the organic composition of capital. Let us assume that the value of production $C+V+S$ goes from $100C+100V+100S$ to $200C+100V+100S$. The organic composition of capital will therefore go from 100 to 200 per cent, the profit rate will fall from 50 to 33 per cent. But if at the same time the surplus-value goes from 100 to 150, that is to say, the surplus-value rate goes from 100 to 150 per cent, then the profit rate $\frac{150}{300}$ remains at 50 per cent: the increase in the surplus-value rate neutralizes the effect of the increase in the organic composition of capital.

Can these two movements occur in exactly the necessary proportions for them to neutralize each other? Here we touch the basic weakness, the Achilles heel of the capitalist system. These two movements cannot develop proportionally over the long run. There is no limit whatever to the increase in the organic composition of capital. For V there is a theoretical limit of zero, assuming the arrival of total automation. But can $\frac{S}{V}$ also increase in an unlimited way, without any limit whatever? No, for in order to produce surplus-value it is necessary to have working workers, and this being the case, the fraction of the workday in which the worker reproduces his own wage cannot fall to zero. It can be reduced from 8 hours to 7, from 7 hours to 6, from 6 hours to 5, from 5 hours to 4, from 4 hours to 3, from 3 hours to 2, from 2 hours to 1, from 1 hour to 50 minutes. It would already be a fantastic productivity which would permit the worker to produce the counter-value of his entire wage in 50 minutes. But he could never reproduce the counter-value of his wage in zero minutes and zero seconds. There is a residual which capitalist exploitation can never suppress.

This means that in the long run the fall in the average rate of profit is inevitable, and I personally believe, contrary to the idea of quite a few Marxists, that this fall is also demonstrable in statistics, that is to say, that the average rates of profit today in the big capitalist countries are much lower than they were 50, 100 or 150 years ago.

Of course, if we examine shorter periods, there are fluctuations up and down; there are numerous factors which come into play (we will discuss them later, when dealing with neo-capitalism). But for the long run, the movement is very clear, both for interest rates and profit rates. We should point out, moreover, that among all the developmental tendencies of capitalism, this was the one most clearly perceived by the theoreticians of capitalism themselves. Ricardo speaks of it; John Stuart Mill stresses it; Keynes is highly aware of it. There was a maxim in England at the end of the nineteenth century which was practically a popular saying: capitalism can withstand anything except a fall in the average interest rate to 2 per cent, because that would kill investment incentive.

This maxim obviously contains a certain kind of error in its reasoning. Calculations of percentages, of profit rates, have a real value, but it is still, after all, a relative one to a capitalist. What interests him is not exclusively the percentage he makes on his capital, but also the total amount which he makes. And if the 2 per cent applies not to $100,000 but to $100 million, it still represents $2 million, and the capitalist would do an awful lot of thinking before he would say that he preferred to let his capital lie idle rather than to accept the revolting profit of a mere $2 million a year.

In practice, we see therefore that there is no total halt in investment activity following a fall in the profit and interest rates but rather a slowing down proportional to the fall in profit rate in an industrial branch. On the other hand, when there is more rapid expansion and a rising tendency of the profit rate in certain industrial branches or in certain periods, then investment activity resumes, speeds up, the movement then seems to feed on itself, and the expansion appears to have no limits up to the time when the tendency reverses once more.

THE FUNDAMENTAL CONTRADICTION IN THE CAPITALIST SYSTEM AND THE PERIODIC CRISES OF OVERPRODUCTION

Capitalism has the tendency to extend production without limits, to extend its arena of activity over the whole world, to view all human beings as potential customers. (Parenthetically, there is a pretty contradiction worth stressing, one which Marx already mentioned: each capitalist always likes to see other capitalists increase the wages of their workers, because the wages of those workers are purchasing power for the goods of the capitalist in question. But he cannot allow the wages of his own workers to increase, for this would obviously reduce his own profit.)

The world is consequently structured in a most extraordinary way, having become an economic unit with an interdependence of its different parts which is extremely sensitive. You know all the cliches which have been used to depict this: if someone sneezes on the New York Stock Exchange, 10,000 peasants are ruined in Malaya.

Capitalism produces an extraordinary interdependence in incomes and a unification in tastes for all human beings. Man has suddenly become conscious of the wealth of human possibilities, whereas in precapitalist society, he was enclosed in the narrow natural possibilities of a single region. In the Middle Ages, pineapples were not eaten in

Europe, only locally grown fruits, but today we eat fruits which may have been produced anywhere in the world and are even beginning to eat fruits from China and India which we were not accustomed to eating prior to the second world war.

There are consequently mutual links being established among products and among men. Expressed in other terms, there is a *progressive socialization of all economic life,* which is becoming a single assemblage, a single fabric. But this whole movement of interdependence is simply centered in an insane way around private property, private appropriation, by a small number of capitalists whose private interests, moreover, collide more and more with the interests of the billions of human beings included in this assemblage.

It is in the economic crises that the contradiction between the progressive socialization of production and the private appropriation which serves as its driving power and its support, breaks out in the most extraordinary way. For capitalist economic crises are incredible phenomena like nothing ever seen before. They are not crises of *scarcity,* like all precapitalist crises; they are crises of *overproduction.* The unemployed die of hunger not because there is too little to eat but because there is relatively too great a supply of foodstuffs.

At first sight the thing seems incomprehensible. How can anyone die because there is a surplus of food, because there is a surplus of goods? But the mechanism of the capitalist system makes this seeming paradox understandable. Goods which do not find buyers not only do not realize their surplus-value but they do not even return their invested capital. The slump in sales therefore forces businessmen to suspend their operations. They are therefore forced to lay off their workers. And since the laid-off workers have no reserves, since they can subsist only when they are selling their labor-power, unemployment obviously condemns them to the starkest poverty and precisely because the relative abundance of goods has resulted in a slump in sales.

The factor of periodic economic crises is inherent in the capitalist system and remains unsurmountable. We shall see further on that this remains equally true in the neo-capitalist regime in which we are now living, even if these crises are now called "recessions." Crises are the clearest manifestation of the fundamental contradiction in the system and a periodic reminder that it is condemned to die sooner or later. But it will never die automatically. It will always be necessary to give it a conscious little push to effect its demise, and it is our job, the job of the working-class movement, to do the pushing.

3

Neo-capitalism

THE ORIGINS OF NEO-CAPITALISM

The great economic crisis of 1929 first changed the attitude of the bourgeoisie and its ideologists toward the state; subsequently it changed the attitude of this same bourgeoisie toward the future of its own system.

Some years ago a notorious trial took place in the United States, the trial of Alger Hiss, who had been an assistant in the State Department during the war. At Hiss's trial, one of his most intimate friends, a journalist for the Luce publications named Whittaker Chambers, was the key witness in his conviction for perjury, actually as a Communist who had allegedly stolen documents from the State Department and passed them on to the Soviet Union. This Chambers, who was somewhat neurotic, had been a Communist during the first ten years of his adult life and wound up as religious editor of the weekly magazine *Time*. He wrote a lengthy confessional under the title *Witness*. In this book there is a passage stating approximately the following concerning the 1929–1939 period: "In Europe the workers are socialist and the bourgeoisie are conservatives; in America, the middle classes are conservatives, the workers are democrats, and the bourgeoisie are communists."

It is obviously absurd to present things in this outrageous way. But there can be no doubt that the year 1929 and the period following the great crisis of 1929–1932 was a traumatic experience for the American bourgeoisie which had been the only one in the whole worldwide capitalist class to be imbued with a complete, blind confidence in the future of the "free enterprise" system. It suffered a terrible shock during this 1929–1932 crisis, a period which was in general the equivalent for American society, so far as becoming conscious of the social question and questioning the capitalist system are concerned, to the period Europe went through at the birth of the socialist workers' movement, the period from 1865 to 1890 in the past century.

For the bourgeoisie, this questioning of the system took various forms on the world scale. It took the form of an attempt to consolidate capitalism by means of fascism and other authoritarian experiments in certain Western, Central and Southern European countries. It took a less violent form in the United States, and it is this American society of the years 1932–1940 which foreshadows what is called neo-capitalism today.

Why is it that it was not an extended and generalized fascist experience which gave neo-capitalism its fundamental characteristic but rather the experiment of an "idyllic detente" in social tensions? The fascist system was a regime of extreme social, economic and political crisis, of extreme tensions in class relationships, which, in the final analysis, was determined by a long period of economic stagnation, in which the margin for discussion and negotiation between the working class and the bourgeoisie was virtually reduced to zero. The capitalist system had become incompatible with any residue of a more or less independent working-class movement.

In the history of capitalism we can distinguish between its periodic crises which recur every 5, 7, or 10 years and its cycles of a longer period, which were first discussed by the Russian economist Kondratief and which may be called long-term cycles of 25 to 30 years. A long-term cycle characterized by high growth rates is often followed by a long-term cycle characterized by a lower growth rate. It seems obvious to me that the period of 1913 to 1940 was one of these long-term cycles of stagnation in capitalist production, during which all the successive cycles from the crisis of 1913 to that of 1920, from the crisis of 1920 to that of 1929, were marked by particularly severe depressions because of the fact that the long-term trend was one of stagnation.

The long-term cycle which began with the second world war, and in which we still remain—let us call it the 1940–1965 or 1940–1970 cycle—has, on the contrary, been characterized by expansion, and because of this expansion, the margin for negotiation and discussion between the bourgeoisie and the working class has been enlarged. The possibility has thus been created for strengthening the system on the basis of granting concessions to the workers, a policy which is being practiced on an international scale in Western Europe and North America and may even be extended to several countries in Southern Europe in the near future. This neo-capitalist policy is based on rather close collaboration between an expansive bourgeoisie and the conservative forces of the labor movement and is fundamentally sustained by a rising trend in the standard of living of the workers.

Nevertheless, in the background of this whole development remains the question mark placed over the system, the doubts regarding the future of the capitalist system, and on that level there is no longer any doubt. In all the decisive layers of the bourgeoisie, the deepest conviction reigns that the automatism of the economy of and by itself, the "market mechanism" cannot insure the survival of the system, that it is no longer possible to rely on the automatic internal functioning of capitalist economy, and that a conscious and expanding intervention, more and more regular and systematic in character, is necessary in order to save this system.

To the extent that the bourgeoisie itself is no longer confident that the automatic mechanics of capitalist economy will sustain its rule, another force must intervene for any long-term salvation of the system, and this force is the state. Neo-capitalism is a capitalism whose preeminent characteristic is the growth of intervention by the state into economic life. From this point of view as well, the current neo-capitalist experience in Western Europe is only an extension of the Roosevelt experience in the United States.

To understand the origins of present-day neo-capitalism, however, we must also take a second factor into account to explain the growing intervention in economic life by the state, and that is the *cold war.* More generally this can be viewed as the challenge which the totality of anticapitalist forces have hurled at world capitalism. This climate of challenge makes the perspective of another serious economic crisis of the 1929–1933 type completely intolerable to capitalism. Imagine what would happen in Germany if there were five million unemployed in West Germany while a scarcity of labor existed in East Germany. It is easy to see how intolerable this would be from a political point of view, and this is why state intervention into the economic life of the capitalist countries is above all anticyclic, or, if you prefer, *anticrisis* in character.

A PERMANENT
TECHNOLOGICAL REVOLUTION

Let us dwell a moment upon this phenomenon of long-term expansion. Without this the specific neo-capitalism we have witnessed in Western Europe for 15 years is incomprehensible.

This long-term cycle started in the United States with the second world war. In order to understand the causes of this phenomenon we must remember that in most of the other expanding cycles in the history of capitalism we find the same common element repeated: technological revolutions. It is no accident that a cyclical expansion of the same kind preceded the period of stagnation and crisis of 1913–1940. The end of the nineteenth century was an extremely peaceful period in the history of capitalism, during which there were no wars, or practically none, except for colonial wars, and during which a whole series of technological researches and discoveries from the previous phase began to find their application. In the current period of expansion, we are witnessing an accelerated technical progress, a genuine technological revolution, for which the expression "second industrial revolution" or "third industrial revolution" hardly seems adequate. We find ourselves, in fact, before an almost uninterrupted transformation of the techniques of production. This phenomenon is virtually a by-product of the permanent arms race, of the cold war in which we have been involved since the end of the second world war.

In fact, if you carefully examine the origin of 99 per

cent of the technological changes applied to production, you will see that they are military; you will see that these changes are by-products of new techniques which first found their application in the military sphere. It is only later, after a longer or shorter time lag, that they come into the public domain to a certain extent and are applied in the sphere of civilian production.

So true is this fact that the advocates for a French striking force (nuclear force) are using it as a major argument today. They explain that if this striking force is not developed, the techniques which will determine an important part of industrial productive processes in 15 or 20 years will not be known in France, for they will all be the by-products of nuclear techniques and their allied techniques on the industrial level.

Here I do not wish to debate this thesis which I consider unacceptable in other respects; I simply wish to underline that it confirms, even in a somewhat "extremist" fashion, that most of the technological revolutions which we are undergoing in the industrial domain and in productive technique generally are by-products of technical revolutions in the military sphere.

To the degree that we are involved in a permanent cold war, which is characterized by a permanent search for technical changes in the sphere of armaments, we have a new factor here, a so-to-speak, extra-economic source, which feeds continuous changes into productive technique. In the past, when this autonomy in technological research did not exist, when it was essentially a product of industrial companies, there was a major factor which determined the cyclical progress of this research. The industrialist would say: we must slow up innovations now, because we have extremely costly installations which must first be amortized. They must become profitable, their installation costs must be covered, before we can start out on another phase of technological change.

This is so true that economists like Schumpeter, for example, have used this cyclical rhythm in technical revolutions as the basic explanation for successive long-term cycles of expansion, or for long-term cycles of stagnation.

Today this economic motive does not act in the same way. On the military level, no reasons are valid for putting an end to the research for new weapons. On the contrary, the omnipresent danger exists that the enemy will be the first to find a new weapon. There is consequently a real stimulus for permanent research, uninterrupted and practically without any economic consideration (at least for the United States), so that the river flows on with virtually no obstruction. This means that we are passing through an era of almost uninterrupted technological transformation in the sphere of production. You have only to recall what has been produced during the last 10–15 years, starting with the release of nuclear energy and proceeding through automation, the development of electronic computers, miniaturization, the laser and a whole series of phenomena in order to grasp this transformation, this uninterrupted technological revolution.

The term "continuous technological revolution" is now just another way of saying that the renewal period of fixed capital has been shortened. This explains the worldwide expansion of capitalism. Like every long-term expansion in the capitalist system, the limits of the present expansion are determined by the amount of fixed investments.

The rapid renewal of fixed capital also explains the reduction in length of the basic economic cycle. This cycle is normally determined by the age of the fixed capital.

To the extent that this fixed capital is now renewed at a more rapid rate, the length of the cycle is also narrowed.

We no longer have crises every seven or 10 years but instead have recessions every four to five years. We have entered a far more rapid series of cycles of far shorter duration than those which occurred prior to the second world war.

Finally, to conclude this examination of the conditions under which today's neo-capitalism is developing, there is a rather important change taking place on a world scale in the conditions under which capitalism exists and is developing.

On the one hand, there is an enlargement of the so-called socialist camp, and on the other, the colonial revolution. And while the balance, so far as a widening of the "socialist camp" is concerned, effectively represents a loss from the point of view of world capitalism—loss of raw materials, investment opportunities for capital, markets, and on all other levels—the balance, so far as the colonial revolution is concerned, paradoxical as this may seem, has not as yet resulted in a substantial loss to the capitalist world. On the contrary, one of the concomitant factors explaining the scale of economic expansion of the imperialist countries occurring in this phase, is the fact that, insofar as the colonial revolution remains in the framework of the capitalist world market (except where it gives birth to other so-called socialist states), it serves as a stimulus to the production and export of industrial equipment, the products of heavy industry in the imperialist countries.

This means that the industrialization of the underdeveloped countries, neo-colonialism, the development of a new bourgeoisie in the colonial countries, all constitute further supports, together with the technological revolution, for the long-term expansion trend in the advanced capitalist countries. Since these fundamentally have the same effects, they also lead to a growth in production for heavy industry and for the industries engaged in mechanical construction in the manufacture of machinery. A part of this machinery serves for the accelerated renewal of fixed capital in the advanced capitalist countries; another part serves for the industrialization, the mechanization of the newly independent colonial countries.

By approaching the subject in this way, we are able to grasp the deeper meaning of the neo-capitalist phase which we are now witnessing, which is that of a long-term expansion of capitalism, a period which I believe is limited in time, just like similar periods in the past. I do not in the least believe that this period of expansion will last forever and that capitalism has now found the philosopher's stone which will allow it to avoid not only its cyclical crises but also its long-term cycles of successive relative expansion and stagnation. But it is this phase of expansion which now confronts the working-class movement of Western Europe with its specific problems.

Let us now turn to the fundamental characteristics of this governmental intervention into capitalist economy.

THE IMPORTANCE OF ARMAMENT EXPENDITURES

The first objective phenomenon which is a tremendous factor in facilitating the growing governmental intervention in the economic life of the capitalist countries is precisely this permanence of the cold war and this permanence in the armaments race. To say permanence of the cold war, permanence in the armaments race, permanence of an extremely high military budget, is also to say state control of an important part of the national income. If we compare the economies of all the big advanced capitalist countries of today with those of all the capitalist countries prior to the first world war, we immediately see the extremely important structural change which has taken place and which is independent of every theoretical consideration and research. It is a consequence of the rise in the military budget. Whereas prior to 1914 the total state budget took 5 per cent, 6 per cent, 4 per cent, 7 per cent of the national income, the budgets of capitalist states today represent 15 per cent, 20 per cent, 25 per cent or even in some cases 30 per cent of this income.

If for the moment we disregard all considerations of interventionism, the very fact alone of this increase in permanent armament expenses signifies that the state is already controlling an important part of the national income.

I have stated that this cold war may remain permanent for a long period. That is my personal conviction. It is permanent because the class contradictions between the two camps confronting each other on a world scale are permanent. Because there is no logical reason for assuming, whether for the short or long run, that the international bourgeoisie will voluntarily disarm in the face of its global enemies or that the Soviet Union and the United States will reach an agreement which might permit a rapid reduction in these armament expenses by one-half or two-thirds or three-fourths.

We therefore start from the point that permanent military expenses will tend to rise in amount and importance relative to the national income, or to become stabilized, that is to say, increase to the extent that the national income will expand during this phase. And it is the very fact of this expansion in military expenses which creates the important role played by government in economic life.

You may know the article by Pierre Naville published in the *Nouvelle Revue Marxiste* several years ago. In it he reprinted a set of figures presented by the director of the [French] budget in 1956, showing the practical importance of military expenses for a whole series of industrial branches. There are many industrial branches, ranking very high in importance and among the leaders in technological development, which are working mainly on contracts with the state and which would be condemned to an early demise if these state contracts disappeared: aeronautics, electronics, naval construction, telecommunications and even the engineering profession, and of course, the nuclear industry.

In the United States the situation is similar; but to the degree that these leading branches are more highly developed and that American economy is on a larger scale, these branches constitute the economic axis for whole geographic regions. It can be said that California, which is the state undergoing the greatest expansion, is largely living off the American military budget. If the country had to disarm and remain capitalist, it would be a catastrophe for the state of California, where the missile industry, military aviation industry and electronic industry are all concentrated. It is unnecessary to draw a picture to illustrate the political effects of this special situation on the attitude of California's bourgeois politicians: you will hardly find them at the head of the struggle for disarmament!

A second phenomenon of this expanding phase which at first sight appears to be in contradiction with the first is the increase in what might be called social expenditures, that is, everything tied more or less closely to social insurance. These outlays have been constantly increasing in governmental budgets generally, and constitute a significant part of the national income over the past 25–30 years.

HOW CRISES ARE 'AMORTIZED'
IN A RECESSION

This growth in social welfare expenditures is the result of several concomitant phenomena.

There is, first of all, the pressure of the working-class movement, which has always aimed at ameliorating one of the most distinct characteristics of the proletarian condition: *insecurity*. Since the value of labor-power only roughly covers the needs of its current upkeep, every interruption in the sale of this labor-power—that is to say, every accident which interferes with the worker's normal job: unemployment, sickness, disability, old age—casts the proletarian into the depths of poverty. In the beginning of the capitalist system, there was only "charity," private or public, to which the jobless workers could turn in distress, with only insignificant material results and at the price of a terrible blow to his human dignity. Little by little, the working-class movement has imposed the principle of *social insurance,* first voluntary, then compulsory, against these blows of fate: health insurance, unemployment compensation, old-age insurance. And the struggle has finally wound up with the principle of *social security,* which would theoretically cover the wage and salary earner against *all* losses of current earnings.

Then there is a certain interest on the part of the state. The institutions receiving the great amounts used for financing this social security program often have large amounts of liquid funds. They can invest these funds in government obligations, make loans to the state (short-term obligations, as a rule). The Nazi regime applied this technique and it subsequently spread to most of the capitalist countries.

The ever mounting size of these social security funds

has, moreover, brought about a special situation, posing a theoretical and practical problem to the working-class movement. The latter properly considers that all funds paid into the social security fund—either by the employers, or by the state, or by withholdings from the wages of the workers themselves—simply constitutes a part of wages, an "indirect wage," or "deferred wage." This is the only reasonable point of view, and one harmonizing, moreover, with the Marxist theory of value, since everything received by the worker in exchange for his labor-power should in effect be considered the price of that labor-power, regardless of whether it is paid him immediately (direct wage), or later (deferred wage). For this reason, "parity management" (union-employer, or union-state) of social security funds must be considered as a violation of a worker's right. Since these funds belong only to the workers, any unwarranted interference in their management by social groups other than the trade unions must be rejected. The workers should no more allow "parity management" of their wages than the capitalists permit "parity management" of their bank accounts.

But the mounting size of these payments into social security has managed to create a certain "tension" between direct wages and deferred wages, since the latter sometimes reach 40 per cent of the total wage. Many trade-union centers are opposed to further increases in "deferred wages" and want to concentrate on having every new gain in the form of an immediate gain in direct payments to the worker. It must be understood, however, that underneath the fact of the "deferred wage" and of social security lies the principle of *class solidarity*. Actually, the funds for sickness, accidents, etc., are not based on the principle of "individual return," (each one eventually receiving everything he or the employer or the state has paid in for his account), but on the *insurance* principle. Those who do not have accidents pay so that those who do may be fully covered. The underlying principle in this practice is that of *class solidarity*, i.e., the interest of the workers in avoiding the *creation of a sub-proletariat*, which would not only undermine the militancy of the laboring masses (each individual fearing to be driven into this sub-proletariat sooner or later) but would also represent a danger of competition for jobs and its threat to wages. Under these conditions, instead of complaining about the "excessive" scale of the deferred wage, we should demonstrate its *pitiful inadequacy*, for it brings about a terrible drop in the standard of living of most old workers, even in the most prosperous capitalist countries.

The effective answer to the problem of the "tension" between direct and indirect wages is the demand to replace the principle of a solidarity limited solely to the laboring class by the principle of a solidarity widened to include all citizens, the transformation of social security into *national services* (of health, full employment, old age) *financed by a progressive tax on incomes.* Only in this way can the "deferred wage" wind up as a genuinely important increase in wages and a *genuine redistribution of the national income* in favor of the wage earners.

It must be recognized fully that up to now this has not been accomplished on a great scale under the capitalist system, and it is even necessary to pose the question of whether this can be realized without provoking a capitalist reaction of such character that we would soon find ourselves in a period of revolutionary crisis. In point of fact, the most interesting experiences with social security, such as the one introduced in France after 1944 and more particularly, the National Health Service in Great Britain after 1945, were financed to a far greater extent by *taxing the workers themselves* (mainly by increasing indirect taxes and by increased taxation of even modest wages, as in Belgium for example) than by taxation of the bourgeoisie. That is why we have never seen a genuine and radical redistribution of the national income by taxation in the capitalist system; it remains one of the great "myths" of reformism.

There is another aspect to this growing importance of "deferred wages," of social insurance, to the national income of industrialized capitalist countries: it is their *anticyclical characteristic*. Here we find another reason why the bourgeois state, neo-capitalism, is interested in increasing the volume of these "deferred wages." It is because it plays the role of a shock-absorbing cushion in preventing too sudden and too violent a drop in the national income in the event of a crisis.

Formerly when a worker lost his job, his income fell to zero. When a fourth of the labor force in a country was unemployed, the income of wage earners and salaried workers automatically decreased by a fourth. The terrible consequences of this drop in income, this drop in "total demand," for capitalist economy in general has frequently been described. It gave the capitalist crisis the appearance of a chain reaction, which kept on going with terrifying logic and inevitability.

Let us assume that the crisis breaks out in a sector producing machines and that this sector is compelled to close its plants and discharge its workers. The loss of income by the latter radically reduces their purchases of consumer goods. Because of this, there is very soon an overproduction in the sector making consumer goods, which, in its turn, is soon compelled to close its plants and dismiss some of its personnel. Again, therefore, there will be a further drop in the sales of consumer goods, and an increase in inventories. At the same time, the plants manufacturing consumer goods, being hard hit, will reduce or cancel their orders for machines, which will bring about the shutdown of more firms engaged in heavy industry, consequently, the dismissal of another group of workers, followed by a new drop in buying power for consumer goods, with another consequent sharpening of the crisis in the light industrial sector, which will in its turn create new layoffs, etc.

But once a system of effective unemployment insurance has been instituted, these *cumulative effects of the crisis are dampened:* the greater the unemployment compensation, the stronger will be the dampening effect on the crisis.

Let us return to the description of the beginning of the crisis. The sector manufacturing machinery experiences an overproduction and has to lay off some of its personnel. But when the unemployment compensation amounts to let us say 60 per cent of his wages, this layoff no longer means a total loss of income to the unemployed, but only a reduction of 40 per cent in his income. Ten per cent unemployment in a country no longer means an overall drop in demand of 10 per cent but only of four per cent; 25 per cent unemployment now means no more than a 10 per cent drop in income. And the cumulative effect of this reduction (which is figured in academic economic science by applying a multiplier to this reduction in demand) will be correspondingly reduced; the crisis will not hit the consumer goods sector so forcefully; the latter will therefore lay off far fewer workers; it will be able to continue some of its orders for machines, etc. In brief, the crisis does not spread out in the form of a spiral; it is "stopped" midway. Then it begins to be resolved.

What we now call a "recession" is nothing but a classical capitalist crisis which has been abated, particularly by means of social insurance.

In my *Treatise on Marxist Economics*, I cite data on the last American recessions which empirically confirm this theoretical analysis. In fact, according to these figures, it appears that the recessions of 1953 and 1957 began with extreme sharpness and had an amplitude comparable in every respect to the severest crises of capitalism in the past (1929 and 1938). But contrary to these pre–second world war crises, the recession of 1953 and of 1957 stopped expanding after a certain number of months, were consequently stopped halfway, then began to recede. We now understand one of the fundamental causes for this transformation of crises into recessions.

From the standpoint of the distribution of the national income between capital and labor, the mounting size of the military budget has an opposite effect to the similar increase in "deferred wages," since in every case a part of the "deferred wage" always stems from supplementary payments by the bourgeoisie. But from the standpoint of its *anticyclical effects,* the mounting size of the military budget (of public expenses generally) and the mounting size of social insurance play identical roles in "abating" the violence of crises, and gives neo-capitalism one of its special aspects.

Aggregate demand can be divided into two categories: the demand for consumer goods and the demand for producer goods (machines and equipment). The expansion in social security funds makes it possible to avoid an extreme drop in expenditures (in demand) for consumer goods after the outbreak of a crisis. The expansion in public expenditures (especially in military expenditures), makes it possible to avoid an extreme drop in expenditures (in demand) for producer goods. Thus, these distinctive traits of neo-capitalism operate in both sectors, not in suppressing the contradictions of capitalism—crises break out just as they did before, capitalism has not found a means of insuring a more or less harmonious and uninterrupted growth—but in reducing their amplitude and seriousness, at least temporarily.

The framework for this process must be a long-term period of accelerated growth but at the cost of permanent inflation.

THE TENDENCY TO PERMANENT INFLATION

One of the consequences of all the phenomena we have just discussed, all of them anticyclic in their effect, is what may be called a tendency to permanent inflation. This has become an obvious manifestation in the capitalist world since 1940, since the beginning or eve of the second world war.

The fundamental cause of this permanent inflation is the importance of the military sector, of the armament sector, in the economy of most capitalist countries. The production of armaments has this special characteristic: it creates purchasing power in exactly the same way that production of consumer goods or production of producer goods does—wages are paid in plants making tanks or rockets, just as they are paid in plants manufacturing machines or textiles, and the capitalist owners of these plants pocket a profit just like the capitalist owners of steel mills or textile plants—but in exchange for this supplementary buying power, there is no corresponding supplementary merchandise placed on the market. Parallel with the creation of buying power in the two fundamental sectors of classical economy, the consumer goods sector and the producer goods sector, is the appearance of a mass of merchandise on the market place, which is capable of absorbing this purchasing power. In contrast, the creation of purchasing power in the armament sector has no compensatory increase in the mass of merchandise, either consumer goods or producer goods, whose sale can be absorbed by the purchasing power thus created.

The only condition in which military expenses would not be inflationary would be if they were completely paid by taxes, and that in proportions which would permit a continuation of exactly the same ratio between the buying power of workers and capitalists on the one hand and between the value of consumer goods and producer goods on the other[1]. This situation does not exist anywhere, not even in those countries where the tax bite is greatest. In the United States, in particular, total military expenses are not at all covered by taxation, by a reduction in the supplementary buying power, so that there is a corresponding tendency toward permanent inflation.

There is also a phenomenon of a structural nature in capitalist economy in the period of monopoly which has the same effect, namely, the rigidity of prices so far as any decline is concerned.

The fact that the great monopolistic trusts virtually or completely control a whole series of markets, particularly the producer goods and hard consumer goods markets, shows up in an absence of price competition in the classical meaning of the term. Whenever supply is less than demand, prices increase, whereas when supply exceeds

---

1. The formula is not quite exact. For the sake of simplification, we are not taking into account that fraction of the purchasing power of the capitalists which is destined (1) for the consumption of the capitalists themselves, and (2) for the consumption of the supplementary workers who are hired as a consequence of capitalist investments.

demand, prices do not fall but remain stable or fall only slightly. This is a phenomenon which has been noted in heavy industry and in the durable consumer goods markets over practically 25 years. It is moreover a phenomenon tendentially linked to the long-term cycle previously discussed, for it must be frankly acknowledged that we cannot predict changes in the prices of durable consumer goods after the close of this long-term period of expansion.

It cannot be excluded that when the automobile industry will increase its excess productive capacity, this will wind up with a new competitive struggle over prices and with spectacular declines. It is possible to defend the thesis that the famous automobile crisis predicted for the second half of this decade (1965, 1966, 1967), could be absorbed relatively easily in Western Europe, if the selling price of small cars was lowered by one half. If the day came that a Citroen 4CV or a 2CV would sell for 200,000 or 250,000 old francs, there would then be such an increase in demand that this excess capacity would most likely disappear in a normal way. This does not appear possible within the framework of present agreements, but if we view the matter in terms of a long period of five or six years of cutthroat competition, something entirely possible in the European automobile industry, then the eventuality cannot be excluded.

Let us immediately add that there is a more likely eventuality, one in which excess productive capacity is suppressed by the shutting down and disappearance of a whole set of firms, in which case the disappearance of this excess capacity will prevent any important drop in prices. That is the normal reaction to such a situation in the system of monopoly capitalism. The other reaction must not be completely excluded, but up to this time we have not witnessed it in any sphere. In the oil industry, for example, the phenomenon of potential overproduction has existed for six years, but the lowering of prices permitted by the big trusts, which operate at profit rates of 100 per cent and 150 per cent, is a drop in the bucket: the price reductions amount to 5 or 6 per cent, whereas the trusts could reduce the price on gasoline by 50 per cent if they wanted to.

'ECONOMIC PLANNING'

The other side of the neo-capitalist coin has to do with the body of phenomena which has been summed up in the terms "managed economy," "economic programming," or still further "indicative planning." It is another form of conscious intervention in the economy, contrary to the classical spirit of capitalism, but it is an intervention which is characterized by the fact that it is no longer mainly a governmental act but is more an act of collaboration, of integration, between government on one side and capitalist groups on the other.

How can we explain this general tendency to "indicative planning," to "economic programming," or to a "managed economy"?

We must start from a real need of big capital, a need which derives from precisely the phenomenon which we described in the first part of our discussion. We spoke there of an acceleration in the rhythm of the renewal of mechanical installations; or a more or less permanent technological revolution. But when we speak of an acceleration in the rhythm of renewal of fixed capital we can only be referring to the necessity of amortizing continuously expanding investment expenses in periods of time which continuously become shorter. Certainly this amortization must be planned and calculated in the most accurate way possible, so as to preserve the economy from short-term fluctuations, which contain the danger of creating incredible disorder in enterprises operating with millions of dollars. This fundamental fact is the cause of capitalist economic programming for its drive toward a managed economy.

Today's capitalism of the great monopolies assembles tens of millions of dollars in investments which have to be amortized speedily. It can no longer afford to run the risk of substantial periodic fluctuations. It consequently requires a guarantee that its amortization costs will be covered and assurance that its revenue will continue, at least for average periods of time corresponding more or less to the amortization period of its fixed capital, periods which now extend between four and five years.

Moreover, the phenomenon has emerged directly from within the capitalist enterprise itself, in which the ever increasing complexity of the productive process implies increasingly precise *planning* efforts in order for it to function as a whole. Capitalist programming is, in the last analysis, nothing but the extension, or more exactly, the coordination on a national level of what has already been happening on the level of the large capitalist enterprise or capitalist groupings such as the trust or cartel embracing a group of companies.

What is the fundamental characteristic of this indicative planning? It is essentially different in nature from socialist planning. *It is not mainly concerned with setting up a set of objectives in production figures and insuring the attainment of these goals.* Its major concern is with coordinating the investment plans already drawn up by private firms and with effecting this necessary coordination by proposing, at the very most, certain objectives considered to have priority on the governmental level. These are, of course, objectives corresponding to the general interest of the bourgeois class.

In a country like Belgium or Great Britain, the operation has been effected in a pretty crude way; in France, where everything happens on a much more refined intellectual level, and a great deal of camouflage is used, the class nature of the mechanism is less obvious. It is nonetheless identical with that of the economic programming of the other capitalist countries. In essence, the activity of "planning commissions," of "planning bureaus," of "programming bureaus," consists of consulting representatives of various employer groups, examining their investment projects and market forecasts, and "harmonizing" the forecasts of the different sectors with each other, and endeavoring to avoid bottlenecks and duplications.

Gilbert Mathieu published three good articles on this subject in *Le Monde* (March 2, 3 and 6, 1962), in which he pointed out that as against 280 trade unionists who have participated in the work of the different planning commissions and subcommissions, there were 1,280 company heads or representatives of employer associations. "In practice, Mr. Francois Perroux believes, the French plan is often set up and put into operation under the preponderant influence of the big companies and financial institutions." And Le Brun, although one of the most moderate trade-union leaders, asserts that French planning "is essentially arranged between the higher agents of capital and the higher civil servants, the former normally having greater weight than the latter."

This confrontation and coordination of the decisions of firms is, moreover, very useful for capitalist entrepreneurs; it constitutes a kind of sounding out of the market on a national scale and over a long term, something very difficult to achieve with present techniques. But the basis for all these studies, all these calculations, still remains the figures advanced as forecasts by the employers.

There are consequently two characteristic fundamental aspects to this kind of programming or "indicative planning."

On the one hand, it is narrowly centered on the interests of the employers which are the initial element in the calculation. And when we say employers, we do not mean all employers, but rather the dominant layers of the bourgeois class, that is to say, the monopolies and trusts. To the degree that a conflict of interest between very powerful monopolies may sometimes arise (remember the 1962 conflict in America between the steel producer trusts and the steel consumer trusts regarding steel prices), the government plays a certain role as arbitrator between capitalist groups. It is, in some respects, an administrative council of the bourgeois class acting in behalf of all stockholders, of all members of the bourgeois class, but in the interest of the dominant group rather than in the interests of democracy and the larger number.

On the other hand, there is an uncertainty lying at the base of all of these calculations, an uncertainty arising from the fact that the programming is based purely on forecasts and from the additional fact that the government has no means for carrying out such programming. As a matter of fact, neither do the private interests have any way of assuring the fulfillment of their forecasts.

In 1956–60, the "programmers" of the Communaute Europeenne du Charbon et de l'Acier [European Coal and Steel Community] as well as those of the Belgian Ministry of Economic Affairs, twice missed the mark badly in their forecasts of coal consumption for Western Europe and especially for Belgium. The first time, prior to and during the crisis in supplies caused by the Suez events, they forecast a substantial increase in consumption for 1960 and a consequent increase in coal production, with Belgian production going from 30 million tons of coal annually to 40 million tons. In reality, it fell from 30 to 20 million tons during 1960; the "programmers" had consequently committed a compound error of rather significant proportions. But no sooner was this one on record when they made another in the opposite direction. While this drop in coal consumption was occurring, they predicted that the trend would continue and declared that it was also necessary to continue closing coal mines. However, the contrary took place between 1960 and 1963: Belgian consumption of coal went from 20 to 25 million tons a year, with the result that after having cut down Belgian productive capacity in coal by one-third, there was an acute scarcity in coal, particularly during the winter of 1962–1963, and it was necessary to import coal post-haste, even from Vietnam!

This example gives us a vivid picture of the *technique* which the "programmers" must resort to ninety per cent of the time when making their calculations for industrial sectors. It is simply a *projection* into the future of *the present trend,* corrected at best by a factor expressing the elasticity in demand, which in turn is based on forecasts of general rates of expansion.

THE STATE GUARANTY OF PROFIT

Another aspect of this "managed economy," which gives it a particularly dangerous character vis-a-vis the working-class movement, is the idea that "social programming" or "income policies" is implicit in the idea of "economic programming." It is impossible to guarantee the trusts' stability in their expenses and incomes for a five-year period, the time necessary for amortizing their new equipment, without simultaneously guaranteeing the stability of their wage expenditures. It is impossible to "plan costs" if "labor costs" cannot be "planned" at the same time, that is to say, if wage increases cannot be anticipated and contained.

The employers and governments have tried to impose such a tendency on the trade unions in all the countries of Western Europe. The attempts are reflected in prolongation of the term of contracts; in legislation which makes work stoppages more difficult or outlawing wildcat strikes; and in a whole propaganda uproar in favor of "income policies" which are apparently the "only guaranty" against the "threat of inflation."

This idea that we must orient toward "income policies," that the rates of wage increases can be calculated exactly, and that we must in this way avoid the incidental costs of strikes "which bring no return to anyone, neither to the worker nor to the nation"; this idea is also becoming widespread in France. Implicit in it is the idea of deeply integrating the trade unions into the capitalist system. From this angle, trade unionism basically ceases to be a weapon of struggle of the workers for *changing* the distribution of the national income. It becomes a guarantor of "social peace," a guarantor to the employers of stability during a continuous and uninterrupted process of work and the reproduction of capital, a guarantor for the amortization of fixed capital during the entire period of its renewal.

Obviously this is a trap for the workers and the workers movement. There are many reasons why this is so and I cannot dwell on them. But one basic reason flows from the very nature of capitalist economy, of market economy generally, and Mr. Masse, the present director of the French plan, admitted it in a recent speech he made in Brussels.

Under the capitalist system, the wage is the price of labor-power. This price varies around the value of this labor-power in accordance with the laws of supply and demand. What, then, is the normal development in the relationship of forces, in the play of supply and demand for labor, during the economic cycle in capitalist economy? During the period of recession and recovery, there is unemployment, which adversely influences wages, and the workers consequently find the struggle for substantial wage increases a very difficult one.

And what is the phase in the cycle which is most favorable to the struggle for wage increases? It is evidently the phase in which there is full employment and even a scarcity of labor, that is to say, the final *boom* phase, the conjunctural peak or "boiling point."

This is the phase in which the strike for wage increases is easiest and in which the employers have the greatest tendency to grant wage increases even without strikes, under the pressure of labor scarcity. But every capitalist technician of conjunctures will tell you that it is precisely during this phase, from the point of view of "stability," of *remaining within the limits required by the capitalist rate of profit* (for that is always at the bottom of this kind of reasoning!), that it is most "dangerous" to call strikes and get wage increases. For if you increase total demand when there is full employment of all the "factors in production," then the supplementary demand automatically becomes inflationary.

In other words, the entire logic of a managed economy is precisely to avoid strikes and attempted improvements *during the only phase of the cycle in which the relationship of class forces favors the working class.* This is the only phase of the cycle, this phase where the demand for labor greatly exceeds the supply, in which wages can stage an upward leap and reverse the unfavorable tendency in the distribution of the national income between wages and profits at the expense of wages.

This means that the "management" is aimed at preventing so-called inflationary increases in wages during this particular phase of the cycle and simply winds up by reducing the overall rate of increase in wages for the whole cycle. A cycle is then secured in which the relative portion of wages in the national income will have a permanent tendency to fall. It already has the tendency to fall during the period of economic revival, since that is a period of increased profit rate by definition (otherwise there would be no revival!); and if the workers are prevented from correcting this tendency during the peak period, it means that the trend toward a deterioration in the distribution of the national income will be perpetuated.

There is, moreover, a practical demonstration of the consequences of a completely rigid policy on incomes under state control with union collaboration; it has been practiced in Holland since 1945 and the results are a matter of record. There has been a marked decline in the ratio of wages to national income, which is matched nowhere else in Europe, not even in West Germany.

Moreover, there are two decisive arguments on a purely "technical" level against the proponents of an "incomes policy."

1. If you demand on "conjunctural" grounds that increases in wages should not exceed increases in productivity during periods of full employment, why don't you demand even greater wage increases in periods of unemployment? On a conjunctural basis, such increases would be justified at that time since they would stimulate the economy by increasing total demand . . .

2. How can an "incomes policy" be practiced with the slightest effectiveness if incomes from wages are the only incomes which are really known? Does not every "in-

comes policy" demand as a prerequisite *workers' control of production, opening up of company books,* and *the abolition of banking secrets,* if for no other reason that to establish the *exact* income of the capitalists, and the *exact* increases in productivity?

Besides, this does not at all mean that we must accept the technical arguments of the bourgeois economists. It is absolutely wrong to say that increasing wages beyond the increase in productivity is automatically inflationary in periods of full employment. This is true only to the degree that the profit rate is left stable and intact. If we were to reduce the profit rate thanks to a tyrannical intervention against private property, as the *Communist Manifesto* puts it, then there would be no inflation whatever; we would simply take buying power from the capitalists and give it to the workers. The only objection that can be raised is that this runs the risk of slowing down investment. But we can turn capitalist technique against its own authors by telling them that it is not such a bad thing to reduce investment when there is a period of full employment and a boom at its "boiling point"; that on the contrary, this reduction in investments is already on the way at the very moment, and that from the standpoint of anticyclical policy, it is more intelligent to reduce profits and increase wages. This would permit the demand from wage workers, from consumers, to come to the relief of investment in the interest of maintaining the conjuncture at a high level, a conjuncture which is threatened by the inevitable tendency for productive investments to fall off at a certain state.

We can draw the following conclusion from all this: state intervention in economic life, managed economy, economic programming, indicative planning, are not the least bit neutral from the social point of view. They are instruments of intervention into the economy which lie in the hands of the bourgeois class or of the ruling groups in the bourgeois class, and are in no sense arbitrators between the bourgeoisie and the proletariat. The only real arbitration which the capitalist governments carry on is an arbitration between different capitalist groups within the capitalist class.

The real nature of neo-capitalism, of the growing intervention of government in economic life, can be summarized in this formula: more and more, a capitalist system left to its own economic automatism runs the risk of perishing rapidly, and increasingly *the state becomes the guarantor of capitalist profit,* the guarantor of the profit of the ruling monopolistic layers of the bourgeoisie. It guarantees this in the measure that it reduces the amplitude of cyclical fluctuations. It guarantees this by state orders, military or paramilitary, of increasing importance. It guarantees this also by *ad hoc* techniques which make their appearance precisely within the framework of the managed economy. The "quasi-contracts" in France illustrate this. They are explicit guarantees of profit to correct certain disequilibriums in development, either regional in character or between branches of industry. The state tells the capitalists: "If you invest your capital in such and such region, or in such and such branch, we will guarantee you six per cent or seven per cent on your capital regardless of developments, even if your junk proves unsaleable, even if you fail." This is the supreme and clearest form of the state guaranty of monopoly profit but it is not the invention of the French planning technicians, since Messrs. Schacht, Funk and Goering had previously applied it within the framework of the Nazi armament economy and its four-year rearmament plan.

In the final analysis, this state guarantee of profits, like all of the genuinely effective anticyclical techniques in the capitalist system, represents a redistribution of the national income in favor of the leading monopolistic groups through the agency of the state. It is effected by the distribution of subsidies, by tax reductions and by granting credits at reduced interest rates. All of these techniques culminate in a rise in the rate of profit, and, given the framework of a normally functioning capitalist economy, especially in its phase of long-term expansion, this rise in the profit rate obviously stimulates investment and works out according to the expectations of the authors of these projects.

Either one stands squarely inside the framework of the capitalist system on a completely logical and consistent basis, and consequently accepts the fact that the only way to guarantee a constant increase in investments and the industrial upsurge based on such increases in private investments is through increasing the rate of profit;

Or one refuses, takes a socialist position, rejecting the road of increasing the rate of profit, and advocates the only alternative road, which is the development of a powerful public sector in industry, alongside the private sector. This is the road out of the capitalist framework and its logic, and passes over to the arena of what we call structural anticapitalist reforms.

In the history of the Belgian working-class movement in recent years, we have experienced this conflict in orientation which awaits France in the coming years, just as soon as it experiences the first rise in unemployment.

Some socialist leaders whose personal honesty I don't want to question have virtually said, and in as brutal and cynical a manner as I put it just a moment ago: "If you want to reabsorb unemployment in a short period within the existing system, there is no other way to do it than by increasing the rate of profit." They did not add, though it goes without saying, that this implies a redistribution of the national income at the expense of the wage earners. In other words, unless you are out to deceive people, you cannot sermonize for a more rapid economic expansion, which under capitalism implies an increase in private investments; and simultaneously demand a redistribution of the national income in favor of the wage earner. In the framework of the capitalist system, these two objectives are absolutely incompatible, at least for the short and middle range period.

The working-class movement is therefore confronted with a fundamental choice between a policy of reform in the *neo-capitalist* structures, which implies an integration of the trade unions in the capitalist system so that they are transformed into gendarmes for the maintenance of social peace during the amortization phase of fixed capital, and a basically *anticapitalist* policy, with a program of short-term anticapitalist structural reforms.

The fundamental goal of these reforms would be to take away the levers of command in the economy from the financial groups, trusts and monopolies and place them in the hands of the nation, to create a public sector of decisive weight in credit, industry and transportation, and to base all of this on workers' control. This would mark the appearance of dual power at the company level and in the whole economy and would rapidly culminate in a duality of political power between the working class and the capitalist rulers.

This stage in turn could usher in the conquest of power by the workers and the establishment of a working-class government which could proceed to the construction of a socialist democracy free of exploitation and all its evils.

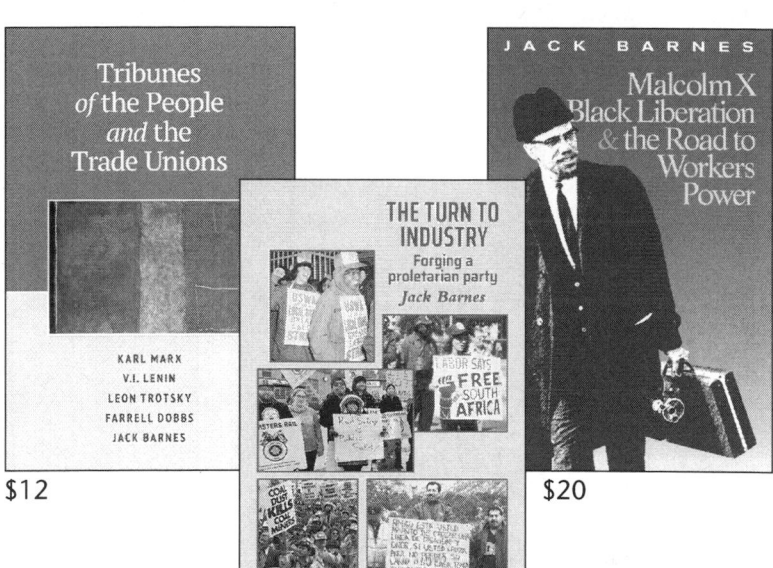

Tribunes
of the People
and the
Trade Unions

KARL MARX
V.I. LENIN
LEON TROTSKY
FARRELL DOBBS
JACK BARNES

$12

THE TURN TO
INDUSTRY
Forging a
proletarian party
Jack Barnes

$15

JACK BARNES

Malcolm X
Black Liberation
& the Road to
Workers
Power

$20

Three books to be read as one . . .

. . . about building the only kind of party worthy of the name "revolutionary" in the imperialist epoch.

• A party that's working class in program, composition, and action.

• A party that recognizes, in word and deed, the most revolutionary fact of our time:

That working people—those the bosses and privileged layers who serve them fear as "deplorables," "criminals," or just plain "trash"—have the power to create a different world as we organize and act together to defend our own interests, not those of the class that grows rich off exploiting our labor. That as we advance along that revolutionary course, we'll transform ourselves and awaken to our capacities—to our own worth.

Three books about building such a party in the US and throughout the capitalist world. Also in Spanish and French.

Special Offer!
All three $30

The Turn to Industry and *Tribunes of the People and the Trade Unions* $20

Either book plus *Malcolm X, Black Liberation, and the Road to Workers Power* $25

FROM THE DICTATORSHIP OF CAPITAL TO THE DICTATORSHIP OF THE PROLETARIAT

The Communist Manifesto
KARL MARX AND FREDERICK ENGELS

Communism, say the founding leaders of the revolutionary workers movement, is not a set of ideas or preconceived "principles" but workers' line of march to power, springing from a "movement going on under our very eyes." $5. Also in Spanish, French, Farsi, and Arabic.

State and Revolution
V.I. LENIN

"The relation of the socialist proletarian revolution to the state is acquiring not only practical political importance," wrote V.I. Lenin just months before the October 1917 Russian Revolution. It also addresses the "most urgent problem of the day: explaining to the masses what they will have to do to free themselves from capitalist tyranny." In *Essential Works of Lenin.* $17

Their Trotsky and Ours
JACK BARNES

To lead the working class in a successful revolution, a mass proletarian party is needed whose cadres, well beforehand, have absorbed a world communist program, are proletarian in life and work, derive deep satisfaction from doing politics, and have forged a leadership with an acute sense of what to do next. This book is about building such a party. $12. Also in Spanish, French, and Farsi.

Lenin's Final Fight
Speeches and Writings, 1922–23

V.I. LENIN

In 1922 and 1923, V.I. Lenin, central leader of the world's first socialist revolution, waged what was to be his last political battle—one that was lost following his death. At stake was whether that revolution, and the international communist movement it led, would remain on the revolutionary proletarian course that brought workers and peasants to power in October 1917. $17. Also in Spanish, Farsi, and Greek.

The History of the Russian Revolution

LEON TROTSKY

How, under Lenin's leadership, the Bolshevik Party led millions of workers and farmers to overthrow the state power of the landlords and capitalists in 1917 and bring to power a government that advanced their class interests at home and worldwide. Unabridged, 3 vols. in one. Written by one of the central leaders of that socialist revolution. $30. Also in French and Russian.

U.S. Imperialism
Has Lost the Cold War

JACK BARNES

The collapse of regimes across Eastern Europe and the USSR claiming to be communist did not mean workers and farmers there had been crushed. In today's sharpening capitalist conflicts and wars, these toilers are joining working people the world over in the class struggle against exploitation. In *New International* no. 11. $14. Also in Spanish, French, Farsi, and Greek.

The US rulers' political crisis and working people's response

Are They Rich Because They're Smart?
Class, Privilege, and Learning under Capitalism
Jack Barnes

Exposes growing class inequalities in the US and the self-serving rationalizations of well-paid professionals who think their "brilliance" equips them to "regulate" working people, who don't know what's in their own best interest. $10. Also in Spanish, French, Farsi, and Arabic.

The Transitional Program for Socialist Revolution
Leon Trotsky

The Socialist Workers Party program, drafted by Trotsky in 1938, still guides the SWP and communists the world over. The party "uncompromisingly gives battle to all political groupings tied to the apron strings of the bourgeoisie. Its task—the abolition of capitalism's domination. Its aim—socialism. Its method—the proletarian revolution." $17. Also in Farsi.

Is Socialist Revolution in the US Possible?
A Necessary Debate among Working People
Mary-Alice Waters

An unhesitating "Yes"—that's the answer given here. Possible—but not inevitable. That depends on what working people *do*. $7. Also in Spanish, French, and Farsi.

The Clintons' Anti-Working-Class Record

Why Washington Fears Working People

Jack Barnes

What working people need to know about the profit-driven course of Democrats and Republicans alike over the last thirty years. And the political awakening of workers seeking to understand and resist the capitalist rulers' assaults. $10. Also in Spanish, French, Farsi, and Greek.

In Defense of the US Working Class

Mary-Alice Waters

"Without understanding the devastation of the lives of working-class families in regions like West Virginia, and the vast increase in class inequality, you can't understand what's happening in the US." But when tens of thousands of West Virginia teachers and school employees set an example in 2018 with their victorious strikes, they drew on the fighting traditions of oppressed and exploited producers of all skin colors and national origins. They fought for dignity and respect for themselves, their families, and for all working people. $7. Also in Spanish, French, Farsi, and Greek.

"It's the Poor Who Face the Savagery of the US 'Justice' System"

The Cuban Five Talk about Their Lives within the US Working Class

How US cops, courts, and prisons work as "an enormous machine for grinding people up." Five Cuban revolutionaries framed up and held in US jails for 16 years explain the human devastation of capitalist "justice"—and how socialist Cuba is different. $10. Also in Spanish, Farsi, and Greek.

EXPAND YOUR REVOLUTIONARY LIBRARY

Malcolm X Talks to Young People

"The young generation of whites, Blacks, browns, whatever else—you're living at a time of revolution," said Malcolm in 1964. "And I for one will join with anyone, I don't care what color you are, as long as you want to change this miserable condition that exists on this earth." Four talks and an interview in Ghana, the UK, and the US in the last months of Malcolm's life. $12. Also in Spanish, French, Farsi, and Greek.

The Teamster Series

FARRELL DOBBS

"The principal lesson from the Teamster experience is not that, under an adverse relationship of forces, the workers can be overcome, but that, with proper leadership, they can overcome." —*Farrell Dobbs* Four books on the strikes, organizing drives, and political campaigns that transformed the Teamsters across the Midwest in the 1930s into a militant industrial union movement. Written by the general organizer of these Teamster battles and leader of the Socialist Workers Party.

A tool for workers engaged in union struggles around wages and conditions, seeking to organize a union in every workplace and advance the fight for an independent labor party. $16 each, series $50. Also in Spanish. *Teamster Rebellion* is available in French, Farsi, and Greek.

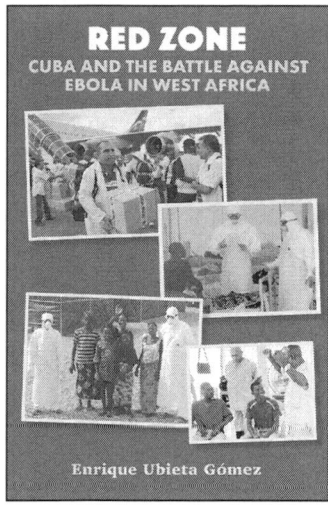

Red Zone

Cuba and the Battle against Ebola in West Africa

ENRIQUE UBIETA GÓMEZ

When three African countries were hit in 2014–15 by the largest Ebola epidemic on record, Cuba's revolutionary government responded to an international call and sent what no other country even pretended to provide: more than 250 volunteer doctors, nurses, and other medical workers. This firsthand account of their actions shows the kind of men and women only a socialist revolution can produce. $17. Also in Spanish and French.

We Are Heirs of the World's Revolutions

Speeches from the Burkina Faso Revolution, 1983–87

THOMAS SANKARA

How peasants and workers in this West African country established a popular revolutionary government and began to fight hunger, illiteracy, and economic backwardness imposed by imperialist domination. They set an example not only for workers and small farmers in Africa, but their class brothers and sisters the world over. $10. Also in Spanish, French, and Farsi.

Capital

KARL MARX

Marx explains the workings of the capitalist system and how it produces the insoluble contradictions that breed class struggle. He demonstrates the inevitability of the revolutionary transformation of society into one ruled for the first time by the producing majority: the working class. Three volumes, $18 each. Also in Spanish.

THE JEWISH QUESTION, THE FIGHT AGAINST

The Jewish Question
A Marxist Interpretation
ABRAM LEON

Why is Jew-hatred still raising its ugly head? What are its class roots—from antiquity through feudalism, to capitalism's rise and current crises? Why is there no solution under capitalism? The author, Abram Leon, was killed in the Nazi gas chambers. This 2020 edition has a revised translation, new introduction, and 40 pages of illustrations and maps. $17. Also in Spanish and French.

The Fight Against Fascism in the USA
Forty Years of Struggle Described by Participants
JAMES P. CANNON

In 1939 some 50,000 people in New York City responded to a call by the Socialist Workers Party to answer a pro-Nazi rally of 20,000. "The question of how to fight fascism was answered in thunderous tones by the magnificent demonstration which raised the cry: Workers Defense Guards to crush the fascist danger!" $5

What Is American Fascism?
JAMES P. CANNON, JOSEPH HANSEN

Analyzes 20th century fascist currents in the US. "A fascist movement if it is to be successful must have a scapegoat on whom the petty bourgeois masses can vent their rage in place of the capitalists who deserve it," wrote Hansen about Father Charles Coughlin's anti-Semitic "Social Justice" movement in the late 1930s. "Coughlin like Hitler and Mussolini has selected the Jew." $5

FASCISM, AND THE WORKING CLASS

Capitalism's World Disorder

Working-Class Politics at the Millennium

JACK BARNES

"Fascism is a movement set in motion by the ruling class to maintain capitalist rule. Not a form of capitalist rule," says Barnes. "When workers understand what fascism really is, then the enormity of the responsibility to combat it becomes that much clearer." $20. Also in Spanish and French.

On the Jewish Question

LEON TROTSKY

"Now more than ever, the fate of the Jewish people is indissolubly linked with the emancipation struggle of the international proletariat," wrote Leon Trotsky. A selection of the exiled Bolshevik leader's writings from the 1930s. $5

The Founding of the Socialist Workers Party

Minutes and Resolutions, 1938–39

JAMES P. CANNON

"The attack against Jews is a spearhead of the attack against the American working class," says a resolution adopted by the 1938 SWP convention. The party demanded that Washington "throw open the doors of the US to victims of the Hitlerite pogrom regime!" $23

New International
A MAGAZINE OF MARXIST POLITICS AND THEORY

Capitalism's Long Hot Winter Has Begun
JACK BARNES

Today's global capitalist crisis is but the opening stage of decades of economic, financial, and social convulsions and class battles. Class-conscious workers confront this historic turning point for imperialism with confidence, Jack Barnes writes, drawing satisfaction from being "in their face" as we chart a revolutionary course to take power. In *New International* no. 12. $14. Also in Spanish, French, Farsi, Arabic, and Greek.

In Defense of Land and Labor
"Capitalist production only develops by simultaneously undermining the original sources of all wealth—the soil and the worker."
—*Karl Marx, 1867.*

THREE ARTICLES

IN *NEW INTERNATIONAL* NO. 13
- **Our Politics Start with the World**
  JACK BARNES
- **Farming, Science, and the Working Classes**
  STEVE CLARK

IN *NEW INTERNATIONAL* NO. 14
- **The Stewardship of Nature Also Falls to the Working Class**
  JACK BARNES, STEVE CLARK, MARY-ALICE WATERS

$14 each issue

CUBA'S SOCIALIST REVOLUTION

Cuba and the Coming American Revolution

JACK BARNES

This is a book about the struggles of working people in the imperialist heartland, the youth attracted to them, and the example set by the Cuban people that revolution is not only necessary—it can be made. It is about the class struggle in the US, where the revolutionary capacities of workers and farmers are today as utterly discounted by the ruling powers as were those of the Cuban toilers. And just as wrongly. $10. Also in Spanish, French, and Farsi.

Women in Cuba: The Making of a Revolution Within the Revolution

VILMA ESPÍN, ASELA DE LOS SANTOS, YOLANDA FERRER

The integration of women into the ranks and leadership of the Cuban Revolution was inseparable from its working-class course from the start. This is the story of that revolution and how it transformed the women and men who made it. $17. Also in Spanish and Greek.

How Far We Slaves Have Come!

South Africa and Cuba in Today's World

NELSON MANDELA, FIDEL CASTRO

Speaking together in Cuba in 1991, Mandela and Castro discuss the role of Cuba in the history of Africa and Angola's victory over the invading US-backed South African army. That victory accelerated the fight to bring down the racist apartheid system. $7. Also in Spanish and Farsi.

WOMEN'S LIBERATION AND SOCIALISM

Origin of the Family, Private Property, and the State

FREDERICK ENGELS

How the emergence of class-divided society gave rise to repressive state bodies and family structures that protect the property of the ruling layers and enable them to pass along wealth and privilege. Engels discusses the consequences for working people of these class institutions—from their original forms to their modern versions. $15. Also in Farsi.

Cosmetics, Fashions, and the Exploitation of Women

JOSEPH HANSEN, EVELYN REED, MARY-ALICE WATERS

How big business reinforces women's second-class status and uses it to rake in profits. Where does women's oppression come from? How has the entry of millions of women into the workforce strengthened the battle for emancipation, still to be won? $12. Also in Spanish, Farsi, and Greek.

Abortion Is a Woman's Right!

PAT GROGAN, EVELYN REED

Why abortion rights are central not only to the fight for the full emancipation of women, but to forging a united and fighting labor movement. $5. Also in Spanish.